PYTHON BUILT-IN FUNCTIONS DICTIONARY

Quick and Detailed Reference for Developers

Kiet Huynh

Table of Contents

Introduction

Whether you are a beginner or an experienced Python developer, having a solid grasp of Python's built-in functions is essential. Python's built-in functions provide ready-to-use capabilities that form the building blocks of the language. Mastering these functions will enable you to write Python code more efficiently and effectively.

This dictionary aims to provide an authoritative, comprehensive and easy-to-use reference to Python's built-in functions. It includes over 100 core functions categorized by purpose, accompanied by clear explanations and usage examples. You will find functions for data types, mathematics, iterables, strings, I/O, code execution and more - all the fundamental capabilities natively available in Python.

With this handy dictionary, answers are never more than a quick lookup away. The organized and condensed format allows developers to rapidly find, understand and apply the built-in functions for their coding needs. Whether you need a quick refresher or a detailed reference, this dictionary will prove an invaluable resource.

Designed for all levels of Python programmers, this dictionary distills the built-in functions down to their essence. The focused coverage cuts through the complexities, providing the essentials you need to boost your productivity with the Python language. Add this must-have reference to your developer toolbox today!

I.
Data Type Constructors

1.1 bool()

Description:

The bool() function in Python is used to evaluate the truthiness or falsiness of an expression or a value. It converts the given argument into a Boolean value (True or False). This function is often used to perform logical checks and comparisons in Python.

Syntax:

bool(value)

- value: The value or expression to be evaluated for its truthiness or falsiness.

Example of Usage:

 # Example 1: Using bool() with non-empty string

result = bool("Hello")

print(result) # Output: True

Example 2: Using bool() with an empty string

result = bool("")

print(result) # Output: False

Example 3: Using bool() with a numeric value

result = bool(42)

print(result) # Output: True

Example 4: Using bool() with 0 (zero)

result = bool(0)

print(result) # Output: False

Example 5: Using bool() with a list

result = bool([1, 2, 3])

print(result) # Output: True

Example 6: Using bool() with an empty list

result = bool([])

print(result) # Output: False

Explanation of the Examples:

1. In Example 1, we use bool() with a non-empty string ("Hello"), and it evaluates to True because non-empty strings are considered truthy in Python.

2. In Example 2, we use bool() with an empty string (""), and it evaluates to False because empty strings are considered falsy in Python.

3. Example 3 demonstrates the use of bool() with a numeric value (42), which is non-zero and therefore evaluates to True.

4. In Example 4, we use bool() with the numeric value 0, which is considered falsy in Python, and it evaluates to False.

5. Example 5 uses bool() with a non-empty list ([1, 2, 3]), which is considered truthy, so it evaluates to True.

6. In Example 6, we use bool() with an empty list ([]), which is considered falsy, so it evaluates to False.

Tips:

- Understanding truthiness and falsiness is crucial in conditional statements (e.g., if statements) and control flow in Python. Values like 0, None, empty sequences (e.g., empty strings, lists, tuples), and False are considered falsy, while all other values are considered truthy.

- When using bool(), keep in mind that it doesn't return the string "True" or "False" but rather the Boolean values True or False.

- You can use bool() in conjunction with conditional statements to check if a value meets a certain condition. For example, if bool(some_value) checks if some_value is truthy, and if not bool(some_value) checks if it's falsy.

- Be cautious when using bool() with complex objects like dictionaries or custom classes. The truthiness of such objects depends on their implementation, so it's essential to understand how they behave in Boolean contexts.

1.2 bytearray()

Description:

The bytearray() function in Python is used to create a mutable sequence of bytes. It is similar to the bytes() function but provides the advantage of allowing you to modify the values of individual bytes within the bytearray. Bytearrays are often used in situations where you need to work with binary data or manipulate bytes directly.

Syntax:

bytearray([source[, encoding[, errors]]])

- source (optional): The source object that initializes the bytearray. It can be a string, bytes, bytearray, iterable, or integer.

- encoding (optional): The character encoding to use when initializing from a string (default is 'utf-8').

- errors (optional): Specifies how encoding errors should be handled (default is 'strict').

Example of Usage:

 # Example 1: Creating a bytearray from a string

text = "Hello, World!"

```python
byte_arr = bytearray(text, 'utf-8')

print(byte_arr)  # Output: bytearray(b'Hello, World!')
```

Example 2: Creating a bytearray from a bytes object

```python
bytes_data = b'\x00\x01\x02\x03'

byte_arr = bytearray(bytes_data)

print(byte_arr)  # Output: bytearray(b'\x00\x01\x02\x03')
```

Example 3: Creating an empty bytearray

```python
empty_byte_arr = bytearray()

empty_byte_arr.append(65)  # Adding the ASCII value of 'A' (65) to the bytearray

print(empty_byte_arr)  # Output: bytearray(b'A')
```

Example 4: Modifying bytes in a bytearray

```python
data = bytearray(b'\x01\x02\x03')

data[1] = 0x10  # Changing the second byte to 0x10

print(data)  # Output: bytearray(b'\x01\x10\x03')
```

Explanation of the Examples:

1. In Example 1, we create a bytearray from a string "Hello, World!" using the 'utf-8' encoding. The resulting bytearray contains the ASCII values of the characters in the string.

2. Example 2 demonstrates creating a bytearray from a bytes object b'\x00\x01\x02\x03'. This creates a bytearray with the same bytes as the input bytes object.

3. In Example 3, we create an empty bytearray and then use the append() method to add the ASCII value of 'A' (65) to it. This shows how to add bytes to a bytearray.

4. Example 4 illustrates how to modify bytes within a bytearray. We create a bytearray with values b'\x01\x02\x03' and change the second byte to 0x10.

Tips:

- Bytearrays are mutable, meaning you can change the values of individual bytes after creating them.

- Bytearrays can be more memory-efficient than strings when working with binary data because they use less overhead for encoding characters.

- When creating a bytearray from a string, you need to specify the encoding. The default is 'utf-8', but you can choose a different encoding if necessary.

- Be careful when working with binary data; make sure you understand the format and endianness of the data you are handling.

- Bytearrays are particularly useful when dealing with low-level network protocols, file I/O, or any situation where you need to manipulate binary data directly.

Description:

The bytes() function in Python is used to create an immutable sequence of bytes. Bytes objects are similar to strings in that they represent a sequence of characters, but they are specifically designed to work with binary data. Bytes objects are immutable, meaning their values cannot be changed once they are created. This function is often used when you need to work with binary data and ensure that it remains unchanged.

Syntax:

bytes([source[, encoding[, errors]]])

- source (optional): The source object that initializes the bytes object. It can be a string, bytes, bytearray, iterable, or integer.

- encoding (optional): The character encoding to use when initializing from a string (default is 'utf-8').

- errors (optional): Specifies how encoding errors should be handled (default is 'strict').

Example of Usage:

 # Example 1: Creating a bytes object from a string

text = "Hello, World!"

```python
byte_data = bytes(text, 'utf-8')
print(byte_data)  # Output: b'Hello, World!'
```

 # Example 2: Creating a bytes object from an iterable of integers

```python
int_data = [72, 101, 108, 108, 111]  # ASCII values of 'Hello'
byte_data = bytes(int_data)
print(byte_data)  # Output: b'Hello'
```

 # Example 3: Creating an empty bytes object

```python
empty_byte_data = bytes()
print(empty_byte_data)  # Output: b''
```

 # Example 4: Creating a bytes object from a hexadecimal string

```python
hex_string = "1a2b3c"
byte_data = bytes.fromhex(hex_string)
print(byte_data)  # Output: b'\x1a+<'
```

Explanation of the Examples:

1. In Example 1, we create a bytes object from the string "Hello, World!" using the 'utf-8' encoding. The resulting bytes object contains the UTF-8 encoded bytes of the string.

2. Example 2 demonstrates creating a bytes object from an iterable of integers representing ASCII values. This results in a bytes object containing the bytes corresponding to the ASCII values.

3. In Example 3, we create an empty bytes object. An empty bytes object is represented as b".

4. Example 4 shows how to create a bytes object from a hexadecimal string using the bytes.fromhex() method. The hexadecimal string "1a2b3c" is converted into the corresponding bytes.

Tips:

- Bytes objects are immutable, so you cannot change their values once created. If you need a mutable sequence of bytes, use bytearray() instead.

- When working with binary data, it's essential to specify the correct encoding when creating a bytes object from a string. The default encoding is 'utf-8', but make sure to choose the appropriate encoding for your data.

- Bytes objects are commonly used when dealing with file I/O, network protocols, or any situation where binary data must be handled directly.

- You can convert a bytes object back to a string using the decode() method, specifying the encoding used to create the bytes object. For example: byte_data.decode('utf-8').

- Be mindful of the data type you're working with. Mixing bytes objects with strings can lead to encoding and decoding issues, so ensure consistent data types when working with binary data.

1.4 dict()

Welcome Description:

The dict() function in Python is used to create a new dictionary object or convert other iterable objects (like sequences or mappings) into dictionaries. A dictionary is an unordered collection of key-value pairs, where each key is unique and maps to a specific value. Dictionaries are highly versatile and commonly used to store and manipulate data in a structured way.

Syntax:

dict(* *kwarg)

dict(mapping, * *kwarg)

dict(iterable, * *kwarg)

- * *kwarg (optional): Key-value pairs separated by commas that are used to create key-value pairs within the dictionary.

- mapping (optional): A mapping object (e.g., another dictionary) whose key-value pairs will be used to create the new dictionary.

- iterable (optional): An iterable object (e.g., a list of tuples) where each item represents a key-value pair.

Example of Usage:

Example 1: Creating a dictionary using key-value pairs

person = dict(name='John', age=30, city='New York')

print(person) # Output: {'name': 'John', 'age': 30, 'city': 'New York'}

Example 2: Creating a dictionary from a list of tuples

pairs = [('a', 1), ('b', 2), ('c', 3)]

dictionary = dict(pairs)

print(dictionary) # Output: {'a': 1, 'b': 2, 'c': 3}

Example 3: Creating an empty dictionary

empty_dict = dict()

print(empty_dict) # Output: {}

Example 4: Creating a dictionary from an existing dictionary

original_dict = {'x': 100, 'y': 200}

copied_dict = dict(original_dict)

print(copied_dict) # Output: {'x': 100, 'y': 200}

Explanation of the Examples:

1. In Example 1, we create a dictionary named person using keyword arguments. The keys are 'name', 'age', and 'city', and the corresponding values are 'John', 30, and 'New York'.

2. Example 2 demonstrates creating a dictionary from a list of tuples. Each tuple contains a key-value pair, and the dict() function converts this list of tuples into a dictionary.

3. In Example 3, we create an empty dictionary called empty_dict with no key-value pairs.

4. Example 4 shows how to create a new dictionary copied_dict by copying the key-value pairs from an existing dictionary original_dict. The result is a new dictionary with the same content as the original.

Tips:

- Dictionaries are versatile data structures that allow you to store, retrieve, and manipulate data using unique keys.

- When using keyword arguments to create a dictionary, the keys become strings automatically, so you can access the values using string keys.

- You can convert other iterable objects like lists, tuples, or sets into dictionaries as long as they contain key-value pairs.

- Be cautious when working with dictionaries because they are unordered collections, which means they don't guarantee a specific order of key-value pairs. If order matters, consider using collections.OrderedDict.

- Keys in a dictionary must be unique. If you add a key-value pair with an existing key, the previous value associated with that key will be overwritten.

- You can access and manipulate dictionary values using square brackets, e.g., my_dict['key'], and you can add or modify values by assigning to a key, e.g., my_dict['new_key'] = new_value.

1.5 float()

Description:

The float() function in Python is used to convert a given value into a floating-point number (float). Floating-point numbers represent real numbers with a decimal point, allowing you to work with both whole and fractional values. This function is commonly used to explicitly convert other numeric types or strings containing numeric representations into floating-point numbers.

Syntax:

float([x])

- x (optional): The value or expression to be converted into a float. If x is not provided, the function returns 0.0.

Example of Usage:

 # Example 1: Converting an integer to a float

integer_value = 42

float_value = float(integer_value)

print(float_value) # Output: 42.0

 # Example 2: Converting a string to a float

```python
numeric_string = "3.14159"

float_value = float(numeric_string)

print(float_value)  # Output: 3.14159
```

 # Example 3: Using float() with no argument (returns 0.0)

```python
zero_float = float()

print(zero_float)  # Output: 0.0
```

 # Example 4: Converting a negative number represented as a string to a float

```python
negative_string = "-7.5"

float_value = float(negative_string)

print(float_value)  # Output: -7.5
```

Explanation of the Examples:

1. In Example 1, we convert an integer (integer_value) into a float (float_value). The resulting float is 42.0, which represents the same numeric value as the integer.

2. Example 2 demonstrates converting a numeric string (numeric_string) containing the value of Pi to a float. The float() function parses the string and creates a float with the value 3.14159.

3. In Example 3, we use float() with no argument, which results in a float value of 0.0.

4. Example 4 shows how to convert a negative number represented as a string (negative_string) into a float. The resulting float is -7.5, representing the negative decimal value.

Tips:

- Be aware of potential exceptions: If you try to convert a string that doesn't represent a valid float (e.g., "abc"), a ValueError will be raised. You should handle such cases or use error-checking mechanisms when dealing with user input or external data.

- When converting from integers to floats, keep in mind that no data is lost. The integer value is represented as a floating-point number with zero decimal places (e.g., 42 becomes 42.0).

- The precision of a floating-point number is limited by the hardware and the IEEE 754 standard, which Python uses for floating-point representation. Therefore, be cautious when comparing floating-point numbers for equality, as small differences may exist due to rounding errors. Consider using a tolerance or epsilon value when comparing floats.

- When converting a string to a float, ensure that the string contains a valid numeric representation and uses a decimal point (.) as the decimal separator (not a comma , in some locales). Use proper error handling to catch and handle conversion failures.

- Floating-point arithmetic may have some quirks due to the binary representation of numbers. It's essential to understand these quirks when dealing with precise calculations. If you need exact decimal arithmetic, consider using the decimal module in Python.

1.6 frozenset()

Description:

The frozenset() function in Python is used to create an immutable frozenset object. A frozenset is similar to a set, but it is immutable, which means its elements cannot be modified after creation. Frozensets are commonly used when you need a set-like data structure that can be used as a key in dictionaries or as an element in other sets.

Syntax:

frozenset([iterable])

- iterable (optional): An iterable (e.g., a list, tuple, or string) that contains elements to be included in the frozenset. If not provided, an empty frozenset is created.

Example of Usage:

 # Example 1: Creating a frozenset from a list

fruits_list = ['apple', 'banana', 'cherry']

fruits_frozenset = frozenset(fruits_list)

print(fruits_frozenset) # Output: frozenset({'cherry', 'banana', 'apple'})

 # Example 2: Creating a frozenset from a tuple

```python
colors_tuple = ('red', 'green', 'blue')

colors_frozenset = frozenset(colors_tuple)

print(colors_frozenset)  # Output: frozenset({'red', 'blue', 'green'})
```

 # Example 3: Creating an empty frozenset

```python
empty_frozenset = frozenset()

print(empty_frozenset)  # Output: frozenset()
```

 # Example 4: Using a frozenset as a dictionary key

```python
person_info = {

    frozenset({'name', 'age'}): {'name': 'John', 'age': 30},

    frozenset({'name', 'city'}): {'name': 'Alice', 'city': 'New York'}

}

print(person_info[frozenset({'name', 'age'})])  # Output: {'name': 'John', 'age': 30}
```

Explanation of the Examples:

1. In Example 1, we create a frozenset fruits_frozenset from a list of fruits. The elements of the list ('apple', 'banana', 'cherry') are included in the frozenset, which is then printed.

2. Example 2 demonstrates creating a frozenset colors_frozenset from a tuple of colors ('red', 'green', 'blue'). The elements of the tuple are used to create the frozenset.

3. In Example 3, we create an empty frozenset empty_frozenset by calling frozenset() with no arguments. The result is an empty frozenset.

4. Example 4 shows how you can use a frozenset as a key in a dictionary. We have a dictionary person_info where keys are frozensets containing sets of attributes, and values are dictionaries containing corresponding attribute values. We access a person's information by using a specific frozenset key.

Tips:

- Frozensets are useful when you need a set-like data structure that is hashable and can be used as keys in dictionaries. Unlike regular sets, frozensets are hashable because they are immutable.

- Since frozensets are immutable, you cannot add or remove elements from them after creation. If you need a mutable set, use the regular set().

- When comparing two frozensets for equality, order of elements doesn't matter. Frozensets are considered equal if they contain the same elements, even if the order is different.

- Frozensets can be used in situations where you want to ensure that a collection of elements remains constant and cannot be accidentally modified elsewhere in your code.

- Frozensets can be converted to other set-like data types (e.g., sets or lists) using set() or list() if you need to modify or work with them in a mutable form.

1.7 int()

Description:

The int() function in Python is used to convert a given value into an integer. It can convert various types of values, including other numeric types, strings representing integers, and floating-point numbers, into integers. This function is commonly used when you need to explicitly convert a value to an integer data type.

Syntax:

int(x, base=10)

- x: The value or expression to be converted into an integer.

- base (optional): The base or radix for interpreting the value of x. The default is 10 (decimal), but you can specify other bases like 2 (binary), 8 (octal), or 16 (hexadecimal).

Example of Usage:

 # Example 1: Converting a floating-point number to an integer

float_value = 3.14159

integer_value = int(float_value)

print(integer_value) # Output: 3

 # Example 2: Converting a string to an integer

```python
numeric_string = "42"
integer_value = int(numeric_string)
print(integer_value)  # Output: 42
```

 # Example 3: Converting a hexadecimal string to an integer

```python
hex_string = "1a"
integer_value = int(hex_string, 16)  # Using base 16 (hexadecimal)
print(integer_value)  # Output: 26
```

 # Example 4: Converting a binary string to an integer

```python
binary_string = "1010"
integer_value = int(binary_string, 2)  # Using base 2 (binary)
print(integer_value)  # Output: 10
```

Explanation of the Examples:

1. In Example 1, we convert a floating-point number (float_value) into an integer (integer_value). The int() function truncates the decimal part, resulting in 3.

2. Example 2 demonstrates converting a numeric string (numeric_string) representing the integer 42 into an integer data type.

3. In Example 3, we convert a hexadecimal string (hex_string) into an integer using base 16 (hexadecimal). The string "1a" in hexadecimal represents the decimal value 26.

4. Example 4 shows how to convert a binary string (binary_string) into an integer using base 2 (binary). The binary string "1010" corresponds to the decimal value 10.

Tips:

- Be cautious when converting floating-point numbers to integers using int(). It simply truncates the decimal part, which can lead to loss of data. If you want to round to the nearest integer, use round() before using int().

- When converting strings to integers, ensure that the string contains a valid integer representation. If the string cannot be interpreted as an integer (e.g., contains non-numeric characters), a ValueError will be raised. Use error handling to handle such cases.

- You can use different bases (e.g., binary, octal, hexadecimal) by specifying the base argument. For example, int('1010', 2) converts a binary string to an integer, and int('1a', 16) converts a hexadecimal string.

- If the base argument is omitted, the int() function assumes base 10 (decimal) by default.

- When using int() with floating-point numbers, it effectively rounds down to the nearest integer. If you want to round to the nearest integer, consider using round() before converting to an integer.

- Be mindful of potential overflow issues when converting very large numbers to integers, as Python integers have arbitrary precision and can represent very large values.

1.8 list()

Description:

The list() function in Python is used to create a new list object or convert other iterable objects (such as tuples, strings, or sets) into lists. Lists are ordered collections of items that can be of mixed data types. Lists are mutable, meaning you can add, remove, or modify elements in the list after creation. This function is commonly used when you need to create a new list or convert an existing iterable into a list.

Syntax:

list(iterable)

- iterable: An iterable object (e.g., a tuple, string, set, or another list) whose elements will be used to create the new list.

Example of Usage:

 # Example 1: Creating a list from a tuple

tuple_data = (1, 2, 3)

list_data = list(tuple_data)

print(list_data) # Output: [1, 2, 3]

 # Example 2: Creating a list from a string

```python
string_data = "Python"

list_data = list(string_data)

print(list_data)  # Output: ['P', 'y', 't', 'h', 'o', 'n']
```

 # Example 3: Creating an empty list

```python
empty_list = list()

print(empty_list)  # Output: []
```

 # Example 4: Creating a list from a set

```python
set_data = {10, 20, 30}

list_data = list(set_data)

print(list_data)  # Output: [10, 20, 30]
```

Explanation of the Examples:

1. In Example 1, we create a list list_data from a tuple tuple_data. The elements of the tuple (1, 2, 3) are used to create the list.

2. Example 2 demonstrates creating a list list_data from a string string_data. The string characters are converted into individual list elements.

3. In Example 3, we create an empty list empty_list by calling list() with no arguments. The result is an empty list.

4. Example 4 shows how to create a list list_data from a set set_data. The elements of the set (10, 20, 30) are used to create the list.

Tips:

- Lists are mutable, meaning you can modify their elements, add new elements, or remove elements after creation. If you need an immutable version of a list, consider using a tuple.

- You can nest lists to create multi-dimensional lists, also known as lists of lists.

- When converting a string to a list, each character of the string becomes a separate element in the list.

- Lists can contain elements of mixed data types, including integers, strings, floats, or even other lists.

- Be cautious when modifying a list while iterating over it using a for loop. It's generally a good practice to create a new list if you need to modify elements while iterating to avoid unexpected behavior.

- Lists are indexed, meaning you can access individual elements by their position (index) within the list. Indices start from 0.

- You can add elements to a list using the append() method, extend a list with another iterable using extend(), or insert elements at a specific position using insert().

- To remove elements from a list, you can use methods like remove(), pop(), or del.

1.9 set()

Description:

The set() function in Python is used to create a new set object or convert other iterable objects (like lists, tuples, strings, or dictionaries) into sets. A set is an unordered collection of unique elements. Sets are commonly used to store a collection of distinct values and perform set operations such as union, intersection, and difference. This function is often used when you need to create a new set or convert an existing iterable into a set.

Syntax:

set([iterable])

- iterable (optional): An iterable object (e.g., a list, tuple, string, or another set) whose elements will be used to create the new set. If not provided, an empty set is created.

Example of Usage:

 # Example 1: Creating a set from a list

fruits_list = ['apple', 'banana', 'cherry', 'apple']

fruits_set = set(fruits_list)

print(fruits_set) # Output: {'apple', 'cherry', 'banana'}

 # Example 2: Creating a set from a string

```python
string_data = "hello"
string_set = set(string_data)
print(string_set)  # Output: {'e', 'o', 'h', 'l'}
```

 # Example 3: Creating an empty set

```python
empty_set = set()
print(empty_set)  # Output: set()
```

 # Example 4: Creating a set from a tuple

```python
tuple_data = (1, 2, 3, 1)
tuple_set = set(tuple_data)
print(tuple_set)  # Output: {1, 2, 3}
```

Explanation of the Examples:

1. In Example 1, we create a set fruits_set from a list fruits_list. The elements of the list ('apple', 'banana', 'cherry', 'apple') are used to create the set. Note that duplicate elements are automatically removed in sets, so only unique elements are present.

2. Example 2 demonstrates creating a set string_set from a string string_data. The set contains the unique characters of the string ('h', 'e', 'l', 'o').

3. In Example 3, we create an empty set empty_set by calling set() with no arguments. The result is an empty set.

4. Example 4 shows how to create a set tuple_set from a tuple tuple_data. The elements of the tuple (1, 2, 3, 1) are used to create the set. Again, duplicate elements are automatically removed.

Tips:

- Sets are unordered collections, which means they do not guarantee any specific order of elements. If you need to maintain order, consider using a list or a collections.OrderedDict.

- Sets are particularly useful when you need to eliminate duplicate values from a collection of elements, as they automatically remove duplicates.

- Sets are mutable, meaning you can add or remove elements after creation. However, set elements themselves must be immutable (e.g., numbers, strings, tuples), as sets are hash-based and rely on immutability for their uniqueness property.

- Be cautious when using sets to ensure you understand their behavior. For example, mathematical set operations like union, intersection, and difference can be performed using set methods or operators (|, &, -).

- To add elements to a set, you can use the add() method, and to remove elements, you can use methods like remove() or discard(). Using remove() on an element not in the set will raise a KeyError, while discard() will not.

- Sets are commonly used in situations where you need to check for membership, eliminate duplicates, or perform set operations like finding common elements between multiple collections.

1.10 str()

Description:

The str() function in Python is used to create a new string object or convert other data types (e.g., numbers, lists, tuples) into string representations. Strings are sequences of characters and are one of the fundamental data types in Python. This function is commonly used when you need to convert data into a string or create a new string.

Syntax:

str(object='')

- object (optional): The object to be converted into a string. It can be a number, list, tuple, dictionary, or any other data type. If not provided, an empty string is created.

Example of Usage:

 # Example 1: Converting an integer to a string

integer_value = 42

string_value = str(integer_value)

print(string_value) # Output: '42'

Example 2: Converting a floating-point number to a string

```python
float_value = 3.14159
string_value = str(float_value)
print(string_value)  # Output: '3.14159'
```

Example 3: Converting a list to a string

```python
fruits_list = ['apple', 'banana', 'cherry']
string_value = str(fruits_list)
print(string_value)  # Output: "['apple', 'banana', 'cherry']"
```

Example 4: Creating an empty string

```python
empty_string = str()
print(empty_string)  # Output: ''
```

Example 5: Converting a dictionary to a string

```python
person_info = {'name': 'Alice', 'age': 30}
string_value = str(person_info)
print(string_value)  # Output: "{'name': 'Alice', 'age': 30}"
```

Explanation of the Examples:

1. In Example 1, we convert an integer integer_value into a string string_value. The str() function converts the numeric value 42 into the string representation '42'.

2. Example 2 demonstrates converting a floating-point number float_value into a string. The float 3.14159 is converted into the string '3.14159'.

3. In Example 3, we convert a list fruits_list into a string string_value. The list is converted into its string representation, including square brackets and comma-separated elements.

4. Example 4 shows how to create an empty string empty_string by calling str() with no arguments. The result is an empty string.

5. Example 5 illustrates converting a dictionary person_info into a string string_value. The dictionary is converted into its string representation, including curly braces and key-value pairs.

Tips:

- The str() function is versatile and can be used to convert a wide range of data types into string representations. However, the string representation may not always be suitable for all purposes. Consider using formatting methods like format() or f-strings (formatted string literals) for more control over the resulting string.

- When converting a numeric value to a string, the resulting string will not contain any leading zeros or special formatting by default. You may need to apply formatting using string formatting techniques if desired.

- Converting data to strings can be helpful when you want to display or print the data, store it in a text file, or concatenate it with other strings.

- Be mindful of the data type you are converting to a string, as some data types may have specific formatting requirements or limitations when converted to strings.

- When converting a collection (e.g., list, dictionary) to a string, the resulting string representation may include special characters and formatting symbols that are specific to Python. Be aware of how this may affect the intended use of the string.

1.11 tuple()

Description:

The tuple() function in Python is used to create a new tuple object or convert other iterable objects (like lists, strings, or sets) into tuples. Tuples are ordered collections of elements that are similar to lists but are immutable, meaning their elements cannot be modified after creation. Tuples are commonly used to group related data items together and represent data structures that should not be changed. This function is often used when you need to create a new tuple or convert an existing iterable into a tuple.

Syntax:

tuple(iterable)

- iterable: An iterable object (e.g., a list, string, set, or another tuple) whose elements will be used to create the new tuple.

Example of Usage:

 # Example 1: Creating a tuple from a list

fruits_list = ['apple', 'banana', 'cherry']

fruits_tuple = tuple(fruits_list)

print(fruits_tuple) # Output: ('apple', 'banana', 'cherry')

 # Example 2: Creating a tuple from a string

string_data = "Python"

string_tuple = tuple(string_data)

print(string_tuple) # Output: ('P', 'y', 't', 'h', 'o', 'n')

 # Example 3: Creating an empty tuple

empty_tuple = tuple()

print(empty_tuple) # Output: ()

 # Example 4: Creating a tuple from a set

set_data = {10, 20, 30}

set_tuple = tuple(set_data)

print(set_tuple) # Output: (10, 20, 30)

Explanation of the Examples:

1. In Example 1, we create a tuple fruits_tuple from a list fruits_list. The elements of the list ('apple', 'banana', 'cherry') are used to create the tuple.

2. Example 2 demonstrates creating a tuple string_tuple from a string string_data. The tuple contains the individual characters of the string ('P', 'y', 't', 'h', 'o', 'n').

3. In Example 3, we create an empty tuple empty_tuple by calling tuple() with no arguments. The result is an empty tuple.

4. Example 4 shows how to create a tuple set_tuple from a set set_data. The elements of the set (10, 20, 30) are used to create the tuple.

Tips:

- Tuples are immutable, which means once created, their elements cannot be changed, added, or removed. If you need a similar data structure that is mutable, use a list.

- Tuples are useful for situations where you want to represent a collection of related values that should not be modified accidentally. For example, coordinates (x, y) or dates (year, month, day) can be represented as tuples.

- When converting a string to a tuple, each character of the string becomes an individual element in the tuple.

- You can nest tuples to create multi-dimensional tuples, which are also known as tuples of tuples.

- Tuples are indexed, meaning you can access individual elements by their position (index) within the tuple. Indices start from 0.

- To access elements of a tuple, you can use square brackets, e.g., my_tuple[0] to access the first element.

- Tuples are hashable, which makes them suitable for use as keys in dictionaries or elements in sets, unlike lists which are not hashable.

II.
Data Type Converters

2.1 ascii()

Welcome **Description:**

The ascii() function in Python is used to return a string containing a printable representation of an object. It converts non-ASCII characters (characters outside the ASCII range) into their escape sequences, making it suitable for producing a string that is safe for ASCII-based output and debugging.

This function is particularly useful when you need to represent non-ASCII characters or control characters in a human-readable format, ensuring compatibility with systems or formats that only support ASCII characters.

Syntax:

ascii(object)

- object: The object that you want to obtain the ASCII representation of.

Example of Usage:

```python
# Example 1: Using ascii() with a string containing non-ASCII characters
text = "Héllo Wörld"
ascii_representation = ascii(text)
print(ascii_representation)
# Output: 'H\xe9llo W\xf6rld'


# Example 2: Using ascii() with a list containing mixed data types
mixed_list = [1, "apple", "ç", True]
ascii_representation = ascii(mixed_list)
print(ascii_representation)
# Output: '[1, "apple", "\\xe7", True]'


# Example 3: Using ascii() with a dictionary containing non-ASCII keys
non_ascii_dict = {"năm": 2023, "été": "summer"}
ascii_representation = ascii(non_ascii_dict)
print(ascii_representation)
# Output: '{"n\\xe2m": 2023, "\\xe9t\\xe9": "summer"}'
```

Explanation of the Examples:

1. In Example 1, the ascii() function is used to obtain the ASCII representation of the string text, which contains non-ASCII characters ("Héllo Wörld"). The non-ASCII characters are replaced with escape sequences, resulting in the ASCII representation 'H\xe9llo W\xf6rld'.

2. Example 2 demonstrates using ascii() with a list mixed_list that contains a mix of data types, including integers, strings, and a non-ASCII character ("ç"). The function produces the ASCII representation, escaping the non-ASCII character as \\xe7, resulting in '[1, "apple", "\\xe7", True]'.

3. In Example 3, a dictionary non_ascii_dict with non-ASCII keys ("năm" and "été") is provided to ascii(). The function returns the ASCII representation of the dictionary with escape sequences for the non-ASCII characters in the keys, resulting in '{"n\\xe2m": 2023, "\\xe9t\\xe9": "summer"}'.

Tips:

- The ascii() function is mainly used for debugging and generating human-readable representations of objects that may contain non-ASCII characters. It can be helpful when you need to ensure compatibility with ASCII-based systems or formats.

- When using ascii() with strings, it will not modify ASCII characters, but it will escape non-ASCII characters with the appropriate escape sequences. For example, the letter "A" remains "A," but the letter "é" becomes '\xe9'.

- When using ascii() with lists or dictionaries, it will apply the function recursively to the elements of the collection, ensuring that all non-ASCII characters within the collection are properly escaped.

- The ASCII representation generated by ascii() can be useful when working with data that may contain characters outside the ASCII range and you need to handle or display them in an ASCII-compatible way.

- Keep in mind that the output of ascii() is a string containing escape sequences. If you want to reverse this process and convert escape sequences back to characters, you can use the str.encode() method with the "unicode-escape" encoding.

2.2 bin()

Description:

The bin() function in Python is used to convert an integer into a binary string representation. It takes an integer as input and returns a string that represents the binary (base-2) value of that integer. Binary representation consists of only two digits, 0 and 1, and is commonly used in computer systems for low-level data manipulation and storage.

Syntax:

```python
bin(x)
```

- x: An integer value that you want to convert into a binary string.

Example of Usage:

 # Example 1: Converting an integer to a binary string

```python
decimal_number = 10
binary_string = bin(decimal_number)
print(binary_string)  # Output: '0b1010'
```

 # Example 2: Converting a negative integer to binary

```python
negative_number = -5

binary_string = bin(negative_number)

print(binary_string)  # Output: '-0b101'
```

 # Example 3: Converting a large integer to binary

```python
large_number = 1234567890

binary_string = bin(large_number)

print(binary_string)  # Output: '0b1001001100101100000001011010010'
```

Explanation of the Examples:

1. In Example 1, we use bin() to convert the decimal integer 10 into its binary string representation. The function returns '0b1010', where '0b' is a prefix indicating that the number is in binary form, and '1010' represents the binary value of 10.

2. Example 2 shows the conversion of a negative integer -5 to binary. The result is '-0b101', where the negative sign is included in the output.

3. In Example 3, a large integer 1234567890 is converted to binary. The binary representation is '0b1001001100101100000001011010010'.

Tips:

- The bin() function is primarily used for converting integers into binary strings for purposes such as low-level programming, bitwise operations, or data storage in binary format.

- The binary string returned by bin() includes the '0b' prefix to indicate that the value is in binary form. You can remove the prefix if it's not needed by using string slicing, like binary_string[2:].

- Negative integers are represented in binary using a two's complement notation, which is why you see a negative sign in the binary string, e.g., '-0b101'.

- Be aware that when converting negative numbers to binary, the binary representation is obtained by converting the positive value to binary and then negating it. For example, -5 is represented as '-0b101' because the binary representation of 5 is '0b101', and then it is negated.

- Python's binary representation uses the least number of bits required to represent the integer value. Leading zeros are not added to pad the binary string.

- You can use the int() function with a base argument to convert binary strings back to integers. For example, int('1010', 2) converts the binary string '1010' to the decimal integer 10.

2.3 chr()

Welcome **Description:**

The chr() function in Python is used to convert an ASCII code (integer representing a character in the ASCII character set) into its corresponding character. It returns a string containing a single character based on the provided ASCII code. This function is often used when you need to generate characters based on their ASCII values.

Syntax:

chr(i)

- i: An integer representing an ASCII code.

Example of Usage:

 # Example 1: Converting ASCII codes to characters

char_a = chr(97)

char_A = chr(65)

char_0 = chr(48)

print(char_a) # Output: 'a'

```python
print(char_A)  # Output: 'A'

print(char_0)  # Output: '0'
```

Example 2: Converting extended ASCII codes

```python
euro_symbol = chr(8364)  # Euro symbol (€)

copyright_symbol = chr(169)  # Copyright symbol (©)


print(euro_symbol)        # Output: '€'

print(copyright_symbol)    # Output: '©'
```

Explanation of the Examples:

1. In Example 1, we use chr() to convert ASCII codes into characters. We convert the ASCII code 97 into the lowercase letter 'a', the ASCII code 65 into the uppercase letter 'A', and the ASCII code 48 into the digit '0'.

2. Example 2 demonstrates converting extended ASCII codes to characters. We convert the ASCII code 8364 into the Euro symbol '€' and the ASCII code 169 into the copyright symbol '©'.

Tips:

- The chr() function is useful when you need to work with characters based on their ASCII values, especially for generating special characters or symbols that may not be directly accessible from the keyboard.

- The ASCII code for uppercase letters ranges from 65 ('A') to 90 ('Z'), for lowercase letters from 97 ('a') to 122 ('z'), and for digits from 48 ('0') to 57 ('9').

- For characters outside the ASCII character set, you can use chr() to generate Unicode characters based on their Unicode code points. Unicode code points are integers representing characters from a wide range of scripts and symbols from various languages and cultures.

- Be cautious when using chr() with large integer values, as it can generate characters that are not printable or may not be supported by all fonts. Unicode code points above 128 often represent characters from extended character sets.

- To convert characters back into their ASCII codes, you can use the ord() function. For example, ord('a') returns 97, which is the ASCII code for the lowercase letter 'a'.

2.4 complex()

Description:

The complex() function in Python is used to create a complex number. Complex numbers consist of a real part and an imaginary part, represented as real + imaginaryj, where real and imaginary are numeric values and j represents the square root of -1. This function is commonly used to create complex numbers for mathematical operations or when working with problems involving complex arithmetic.

Syntax:

complex([real[, imag]])

- real (optional): The real part of the complex number. If not provided, it defaults to 0.

- imag (optional): The imaginary part of the complex number. If not provided, it defaults to 0.

Example of Usage:

 # Example 1: Creating a complex number with real and imaginary parts

complex_num = complex(3, 4)

print(complex_num) # Output: (3+4j)

Example 2: Creating a complex number with only a real part

real_part = 5

complex_num = complex(real_part)

print(complex_num) # Output: (5+0j)

Example 3: Creating a complex number with only an imaginary part

imag_part = -2.5

complex_num = complex(0, imag_part)

print(complex_num) # Output: (-2.5j)

Example 4: Creating a complex number with default values (0 + 0j)

default_complex = complex()

print(default_complex) # Output: 0j

Explanation of the Examples:

1. In Example 1, we create a complex number complex_num with both real and imaginary parts specified as 3 and 4, respectively. The output is (3+4j).

2. Example 2 demonstrates creating a complex number complex_num with only a real part specified as 5. The imaginary part defaults to 0, resulting in (5+0j).

3. In Example 3, a complex number complex_num is created with only an imaginary part specified as -2.5. The real part defaults to 0, resulting in (-2.5j).

4. Example 4 creates a complex number default_complex with no real or imaginary parts specified, so both parts default to 0, resulting in 0j.

Tips:

- Complex numbers are a fundamental data type in Python, and they are often used in scientific and engineering applications for tasks involving complex arithmetic, such as solving mathematical equations that involve square roots of negative numbers.

- You can perform arithmetic operations (addition, subtraction, multiplication, division) with complex numbers just like you would with real numbers. Python's built-in operators work seamlessly with complex numbers.

- To access the real and imaginary parts of a complex number, you can use the .real and .imag attributes, respectively. For example, complex_num.real returns the real part, and complex_num.imag returns the imaginary part.

- Complex numbers are commonly used in mathematical libraries like NumPy and in applications such as signal processing, control systems, and quantum computing.

- When working with complex numbers, be mindful of the j notation for the imaginary part. For example, 3 + 4j represents a complex number with a real part of 3 and an imaginary part of 4.

2.5 hex()

Welcome **Description:**

The hex() function in Python is used to convert an integer into a hexadecimal (base-16) string representation. It takes an integer as input and returns a string that represents the hexadecimal value of that integer. Hexadecimal representation uses digits 0-9 and letters A-F to represent values from 0 to 15, making it useful for displaying binary data or memory addresses.

Syntax:

hex(x)

- x: An integer value that you want to convert into a hexadecimal string.

Example of Usage:

Example 1: Converting an integer to a hexadecimal string

decimal_number = 255

hexadecimal_string = hex(decimal_number)

print(hexadecimal_string) # Output: '0xff'

Example 2: Converting a negative integer to hexadecimal

negative_number = -16

hexadecimal_string = hex(negative_number)

print(hexadecimal_string) # Output: '-0x10'

Example 3: Converting a large integer to hexadecimal

large_number = 4294967296 # 2^32

hexadecimal_string = hex(large_number)

print(hexadecimal_string) # Output: '0x100000000'

Explanation of the Examples:

1. In Example 1, we use hex() to convert the decimal integer 255 into its hexadecimal string representation. The function returns '0xff', where '0x' is a prefix indicating that the number is in hexadecimal form, and 'ff' represents the hexadecimal value of 255.

2. Example 2 shows the conversion of a negative integer -16 to hexadecimal. The result is '-0x10', where the negative sign is included in the output, and '0x' is the prefix indicating hexadecimal form.

3. In Example 3, a large integer 4294967296 (equal to 2^32) is converted to hexadecimal. The hexadecimal representation is '0x100000000', reflecting the large value.

Tips:

- The hex() function is primarily used for converting integers into hexadecimal strings for purposes such as displaying memory addresses, representing binary data, or debugging.

- Hexadecimal strings returned by hex() include the '0x' prefix to indicate that the value is in hexadecimal form. You can remove the prefix if it's not needed by using string slicing, like hexadecimal_string[2:].

- When converting negative numbers to hexadecimal, the function follows two's complement notation, which is why you see a negative sign in the hexadecimal string, e.g., '-0x10'.

- Be cautious when using hex() with large integer values, as the resulting hexadecimal string can be quite long and may not be easily readable.

- Hexadecimal notation is commonly used in low-level programming, such as when working with memory addresses, binary data, or when specifying colors in web design (e.g., HTML/CSS color codes).

- To convert hexadecimal strings back into integers, you can use the int() function with a base argument of 16. For example, int('ff', 16) converts the hexadecimal string 'ff' to the decimal integer 255.

2.6 oct()

Description:

The oct() function in Python is used to convert an integer into an octal (base-8) string representation. It takes an integer as input and returns a string that represents the octal value of that integer. Octal representation uses digits 0-7 to represent values from 0 to 7, making it useful for displaying binary data or permissions in Unix-like systems.

Syntax:

oct(x)

- x: An integer value that you want to convert into an octal string.

Example of Usage:

 # Example 1: Converting an integer to an octal string

decimal_number = 64

octal_string = oct(decimal_number)

print(octal_string) # Output: '0o100'

 # Example 2: Converting a negative integer to octal

negative_number = -8

octal_string = oct(negative_number)

print(octal_string) # Output: '-0o10'

 # Example 3: Converting a large integer to octal

large_number = 536870912 # 8^9

octal_string = oct(large_number)

print(octal_string) # Output: '0o2000000000'

Explanation of the Examples:

1. In Example 1, we use oct() to convert the decimal integer 64 into its octal string representation. The function returns '0o100', where '0o' is a prefix indicating that the number is in octal form, and '100' represents the octal value of 64.

2. Example 2 shows the conversion of a negative integer -8 to octal. The result is '-0o10', where the negative sign is included in the output, and '0o' is the prefix indicating octal form.

3. In Example 3, a large integer 536870912 (equal to 8^9) is converted to octal. The octal representation is '0o2000000000', reflecting the large value.

Tips:

- The oct() function is primarily used for converting integers into octal strings for purposes such as displaying permissions in Unix-like systems, representing binary data, or debugging.

- Octal strings returned by oct() include the '0o' prefix to indicate that the value is in octal form. You can remove the prefix if it's not needed by using string slicing, like octal_string[2:].

- When converting negative numbers to octal, the function follows two's complement notation, which is why you see a negative sign in the octal string, e.g., '-0o10'.

- Be cautious when using oct() with large integer values, as the resulting octal string can be quite long and may not be easily readable.

- Octal notation is not as commonly used as hexadecimal in modern programming but may still be relevant in certain contexts, such as Unix file permissions, where octal values are often used to represent file permission modes.

- To convert octal strings back into integers, you can use the int() function with a base argument of 8. For example, int('100', 8) converts the octal string '100' to the decimal integer 64.

2.7 ord()

Description:

The ord() function in Python is used to obtain the Unicode code point (integer representation) of a character. It takes a single character (a string of length 1) as input and returns the Unicode code point for that character. Unicode code points are integers that uniquely represent each character or symbol in the Unicode character set, which encompasses a wide range of characters from various languages and scripts.

Syntax:

ord(c)

- c: A character (string of length 1) for which you want to obtain the Unicode code point.

Example of Usage:

Example 1: Obtaining the Unicode code point of characters

code_point_a = ord('A')

code_point_1 = ord('1')

code_point_euro = ord('€')

```python
print(code_point_a)       # Output: 65

print(code_point_1)       # Output: 49

print(code_point_euro)    # Output: 8364
```

Explanation of the Examples:

1. In Example 1, we use ord() to obtain the Unicode code points of various characters. The function returns 65 for the character 'A', 49 for the character '1', and 8364 for the Euro symbol '€'.

Tips:

- The ord() function is useful when you need to work with the numerical representation of characters, especially when comparing, sorting, or processing textual data in a way that considers the character's order in the Unicode character set.

- Unicode is a standardized character encoding that supports characters from multiple languages and scripts, making it suitable for internationalization and multilingual applications.

- The Unicode code point for ASCII characters (those in the 7-bit ASCII character set) matches their ASCII values. For example, ord('A') returns 65, which is the ASCII value for uppercase 'A'.

- Be aware that ord() returns an integer representing the Unicode code point, and this integer can be used in various operations, such as arithmetic, comparison, and indexing.

- When dealing with non-ASCII characters or symbols, the Unicode code points can be significantly larger than ASCII values. For example, the Euro symbol '€' has a Unicode code point of 8364.

- Keep in mind that the ord() function expects a single character as input. If you provide a string with more than one character, it will raise a TypeError.

- To convert Unicode code points back into characters, you can use the chr() function. For example, chr(65) returns the character 'A', which corresponds to the Unicode code point 65.

2.8 repr()

Description:

The repr() function in Python is used to obtain a string representation of an object, typically one that is suitable for reproducing the object or debugging. It returns a string that represents the object in a way that, if passed to the eval() function, would create an object with the same value.

The primary purpose of repr() is to provide a human-readable and unambiguous representation of an object. It is often used for debugging and generating string representations of objects that can be used to recreate them.

Syntax:

repr(object)

- object: The object for which you want to obtain the string representation.

Example of Usage:

 # Example 1: Using repr() with integers and strings

integer_value = 42

string_value = "Hello, world!"

```python
repr_integer = repr(integer_value)
repr_string = repr(string_value)


print(repr_integer)  # Output: '42'
print(repr_string)   # Output: '"Hello, world!"'


# Example 2: Using repr() with a list
my_list = [1, 2, 3, "apple", True]
repr_list = repr(my_list)


print(repr_list)
# Output: '[1, 2, 3, "apple", True]'


# Example 3: Using repr() with a custom object
class Person:
    def __init__(self, name, age):
        self.name = name
        self.age = age


person_obj = Person("Alice", 30)
repr_person = repr(person_obj)


print(repr_person)
# Output: '<__main__.Person object at 0x7f9d5efbe790>'
```

Explanation of the Examples:

1. In Example 1, we use repr() to obtain string representations of an integer (integer_value) and a string (string_value). The resulting representations are '42' and '"Hello, world!"', respectively.

2. Example 2 demonstrates using repr() with a list (my_list). The resulting representation of the list includes the list's elements and is suitable for recreating the list.

3. In Example 3, we create a custom class Person and create an instance of it (person_obj). Using repr() on the person_obj provides a representation that includes the object's class name and memory address.

Tips:

- The repr() function is often used for debugging because it provides a clear and unambiguous representation of objects. This makes it easier to identify the state of an object during debugging.

- The string representation obtained from repr() is intended to be a valid Python expression. This means that you can typically use the result of repr() with eval() to recreate the original object. However, be cautious when using eval() with untrusted or unsanitized input, as it can execute arbitrary code.

- The repr() function can be overridden for custom classes by defining the __repr__() method within the class. This allows you to customize the string representation of instances of the class.

- While repr() aims for unambiguous representations, the str() function is used to obtain a more user-friendly string representation. You can override the __str__() method in your custom class to provide a custom string representation when using str().

- The repr() function is useful for logging, debugging, and when you need to display the internal state of objects in a human-readable format. It's a valuable tool for understanding how objects are structured and can help diagnose issues in your code.

2.9 str()

Description:

The str() function in Python is used to create a string representation of an object. It converts a given object into a string, allowing you to work with the object as text. This function is commonly used to convert non-string objects, such as numbers or data structures, into strings so that they can be concatenated with other strings, displayed, or stored as text.

Syntax:

str(object)

- object: The object you want to convert into a string.

Example of Usage:

 # Example 1: Converting integers and floats to strings

integer_value = 42

float_value = 3.14159

str_integer = str(integer_value)

str_float = str(float_value)

```python
print(str_integer)  # Output: '42'
print(str_float)    # Output: '3.14159'


# Example 2: Converting a list to a string
my_list = [1, 2, 3, "apple", True]
str_list = str(my_list)


print(str_list)
# Output: '[1, 2, 3, "apple", True]'


# Example 3: Converting a custom object to a string
class Person:
    def __init__(self, name, age):
        self.name = name
        self.age = age


person_obj = Person("Alice", 30)
str_person = str(person_obj)


print(str_person)  # Output: '<__main__.Person object at 0x7f9d5efbe790>'
```

Explanation of the Examples:

1. In Example 1, we use str() to convert an integer (integer_value) and a float (float_value) into string representations. The resulting strings are '42' and '3.14159', respectively.

2. Example 2 demonstrates using str() with a list (my_list). The list is converted into a string representation that includes the list's elements.

3. In Example 3, we create a custom class Person and create an instance of it (person_obj). Using str() on the person_obj provides a string representation that includes the object's class name and memory address.

Tips:

- The str() function is a versatile tool for converting various objects into strings. It is commonly used in Python for formatting output, logging, and displaying data as text.

- When used with custom classes, the str() function will provide a default representation that may not be very informative. You can customize the string representation of objects by defining the __str__() method within the class.

- Keep in mind that the string representation produced by str() aims to be human-readable. It may not always be suitable for recreating the original object. For that purpose, consider using the repr() function.

- The str() function is often used with the print() function to display objects as text in the console or when writing to text files.

- When working with non-string objects, you can concatenate them with other strings using the + operator after converting them to strings with str(). For example, message = "Value: " + str(42) combines the string "Value: " with the string representation of the integer 42.

- Be aware that not all objects can be directly converted into strings. Some objects may raise a TypeError if used with str() if they don't support string conversion.

III.
Mathematical Functions

3.1 abs()

Description:

The abs() function in Python is used to obtain the absolute value of a number. It returns the non-negative value of a given number, which is the distance of that number from zero on the number line. In other words, it removes the sign of the number, making it positive if it was negative.

Syntax:

abs(x)

- x: The number for which you want to obtain the absolute value.

Example of Usage:

Example 1: Using abs() with integers and floats

```python
integer_value = -42

float_value = -3.14159


abs_integer = abs(integer_value)

abs_float = abs(float_value)


print(abs_integer)  # Output: 42

print(abs_float)    # Output: 3.14159
```

Example 2: Using abs() with complex numbers

```python
complex_number = -2 + 3j

abs_complex = abs(complex_number)


print(abs_complex)  # Output: 3.605551275463989
```

Example 3: Using abs() with lists

```python
list_of_numbers = [-1, -2, 3, -4, 5]

abs_list = [abs(num) for num in list_of_numbers]


print(abs_list)  # Output: [1, 2, 3, 4, 5]
```

Explanation of the Examples:

1. In Example 1, we use abs() to obtain the absolute values of both an integer (integer_value) and a float (float_value). The function removes the negative sign from both numbers, resulting in 42 and 3.14159, respectively.

2. Example 2 demonstrates using abs() with a complex number (complex_number). The absolute value of a complex number is the magnitude or distance from the origin in the complex plane. The result is approximately 3.605551275463989.

3. In Example 3, we use a list comprehension to apply abs() to each element in a list of numbers (list_of_numbers). This results in a new list (abs_list) containing the absolute values of the original numbers.

Tips:

- The abs() function is useful when you need to obtain the magnitude or distance of a number from zero, regardless of whether the number is positive or negative.

- While abs() is commonly used with real numbers (integers and floats), it can also be used with complex numbers to obtain their magnitudes.

- When applying abs() to a complex number, it calculates the square root of the sum of the squares of the real and imaginary parts. This results in a non-negative real number.

- When working with collections of numbers, you can use list comprehensions or other iterative methods to apply abs() to each element, as shown in Example 3.

- Be cautious when using abs() with objects that are not numbers or complex numbers, as it may not produce meaningful results. It is primarily intended for numerical data.

3.2 divmod()

Description:

The divmod() function in Python is used to perform both division and modulus (remainder) operations on two numbers simultaneously and returns a tuple containing the quotient and the remainder. It provides an efficient way to obtain both results in a single function call.

Syntax:

divmod(a, b)

- a: The dividend, the number to be divided.

- b: The divisor, the number by which the dividend is divided.

Example of Usage:

 # Example 1: Using divmod() with integers

result = divmod(10, 3)

print(result) # Output: (3, 1)

 # Example 2: Using divmod() with floats

result = divmod(8.5, 2.5)

print(result) # Output: (3.0, 0.5)

Example 3: Using divmod() with negative numbers

result = divmod(-11, 4)

print(result) # Output: (-3, 1)

Explanation of the Examples:

1. In Example 1, we use divmod() to perform division and modulus operations on the integers 10 and 3. The result is a tuple (3, 1), where 3 is the quotient of 10 divided by 3, and 1 is the remainder.

2. Example 2 demonstrates using divmod() with floating-point numbers 8.5 and 2.5. The result is a tuple (3.0, 0.5), where 3.0 is the quotient of 8.5 divided by 2.5, and 0.5 is the remainder.

3. In Example 3, we use divmod() with negative numbers (-11) and 4. The result is a tuple (-3, 1), where -3 is the quotient of -11 divided by 4, and 1 is the remainder. Note that the quotient has the same sign as the dividend.

Tips:

- divmod() is particularly useful when you need both the quotient and the remainder of a division operation. It can help optimize code by avoiding the need to perform two separate operations.

- The result of divmod() is always returned as a tuple with two elements: the quotient (integer division result) and the remainder. Both elements of the tuple have the same sign as the dividend.

- You can use tuple unpacking to conveniently assign the quotient and remainder to separate variables, like this:

```
quotient, remainder = divmod(10, 3)
```

- When working with non-integer numbers, the result of divmod() includes a floating-point quotient if either the dividend or divisor is a float.

- Be cautious when using divmod() with divisor values of 0, as it will raise a ZeroDivisionError since division by zero is undefined.

3.3 max()

Description:

The max() function in Python is used to find the maximum value among the elements in an iterable (such as a list, tuple, or string) or among a set of provided values. It returns the largest element from the input, allowing you to find the maximum value within a collection or compare values to determine the maximum.

Syntax:

max(iterable, *iterables, key=None, default=object)

- iterable: The iterable or collection from which you want to find the maximum element.

- *iterables: Additional iterables or collections to compare if needed.

- key (optional): A function that calculates a custom key for each element and is used for comparison. (Default is None.)

- default (optional): A value to return if the iterable is empty, or if there is no maximum element. (Default is object, which raises an exception if used.)

Example of Usage:

 # Example 1: Finding the maximum element in a list

```python
numbers = [3, 9, 1, 5, 7]
max_number = max(numbers)
print(max_number)  # Output: 9
```

 # Example 2: Finding the maximum element in a tuple

```python
fruits = ("apple", "banana", "cherry", "date")
longest_fruit = max(fruits, key=len)
print(longest_fruit)  # Output: "banana"
```

 # Example 3: Finding the maximum value from multiple iterables

```python
list1 = [12, 45, 67]
list2 = [23, 56, 89]
list3 = [34, 78, 9]
max_value = max(list1, list2, list3)
print(max_value)  # Output: 89
```

Explanation of the Examples:

1. In Example 1, we use max() to find the maximum element in a list of numbers (numbers). The maximum value 9 is returned.

2. Example 2 shows finding the maximum element in a tuple of strings (fruits). We use the key argument to specify the len function as the key, which calculates the length of each string. As a result, the longest string, "banana," is returned.

3. In Example 3, we find the maximum value among multiple lists (list1, list2, list3) by passing them as separate arguments to max(). The maximum value 89 from list2 is returned.

Tips:

- The max() function is versatile and can be used with a variety of iterable data types, including lists, tuples, strings, and even custom objects, provided that appropriate comparison logic is defined.

- If you want to find the maximum element based on some custom criterion, you can use the key argument, which should be a function that generates a value for each element to be compared. The maximum element is determined based on the values generated by the key function.

- When using max() with strings, it returns the element that comes last in lexicographic (dictionary) order. This means it compares strings based on their Unicode code points.

- Be cautious when using max() with non-numeric data types, as the comparison may not always yield the expected results. In such cases, consider using the key argument to customize the comparison logic.

- If the iterable is empty or if there is no maximum element (e.g., comparing an empty list), max() will raise a ValueError by default. You can specify a default value using the default argument to avoid this exception.

3.4 min()

Description:

The min() function in Python is used to find the minimum value among the elements in an iterable (such as a list, tuple, or string) or among a set of provided values. It returns the smallest element from the input, allowing you to find the minimum value within a collection or compare values to determine the minimum.

Syntax:

min(iterable, *iterables, key=None, default=object)

- iterable: The iterable or collection from which you want to find the minimum element.

- *iterables: Additional iterables or collections to compare if needed.

- key (optional): A function that calculates a custom key for each element and is used for comparison. (Default is None.)

- default (optional): A value to return if the iterable is empty, or if there is no minimum element. (Default is object, which raises an exception if used.)

Example of Usage:

 # Example 1: Finding the minimum element in a list

```python
numbers = [3, 9, 1, 5, 7]

min_number = min(numbers)

print(min_number)  # Output: 1
```

 # Example 2: Finding the minimum element in a tuple

```python
fruits = ("apple", "banana", "cherry", "date")

shortest_fruit = min(fruits, key=len)

print(shortest_fruit)  # Output: "date"
```

 # Example 3: Finding the minimum value from multiple iterables

```python
list1 = [12, 45, 67]

list2 = [23, 56, 89]

list3 = [34, 78, 9]

min_value = min(list1, list2, list3)

print(min_value)  # Output: 9
```

Explanation of the Examples:

1. In Example 1, we use min() to find the minimum element in a list of numbers (numbers). The minimum value 1 is returned.

2. Example 2 shows finding the minimum element in a tuple of strings (fruits). We use the key argument to specify the len function as the key, which calculates the length of each string. As a result, the shortest string, "date," is returned.

3. In Example 3, we find the minimum value among multiple lists (list1, list2, list3) by passing them as separate arguments to min(). The minimum value 9 from list3 is returned.

Tips:

- The min() function is versatile and can be used with a variety of iterable data types, including lists, tuples, strings, and even custom objects, provided that appropriate comparison logic is defined.

- If you want to find the minimum element based on some custom criterion, you can use the key argument, which should be a function that generates a value for each element to be compared. The minimum element is determined based on the values generated by the key function.

- When using min() with strings, it returns the element that comes first in lexicographic (dictionary) order. This means it compares strings based on their Unicode code points.

- Be cautious when using min() with non-numeric data types, as the comparison may not always yield the expected results. In such cases, consider using the key argument to customize the comparison logic.

- If the iterable is empty or if there is no minimum element (e.g., comparing an empty list), min() will raise a ValueError by default. You can specify a default value using the default argument to avoid this exception.

3.5 pow()

Description:

The pow() function in Python is used to calculate the result of raising a number to a specified power or exponent. It computes the exponentiation of a base number to the power of an exponent, optionally with a third argument to specify a modulo operation. This function is useful for performing mathematical operations involving exponentiation and modular arithmetic.

Syntax:

pow(base, exponent, modulus=None)

- base: The base number.

- exponent: The exponent to which the base is raised.

- modulus (optional): An optional value that represents the modulus for performing modular exponentiation. If provided, the result will be calculated as (base * * exponent) % modulus. If None, the regular exponentiation is performed. (Default is None.)

Example of Usage:

 # Example 1: Calculating exponentiation without modulus

result1 = pow(2, 3)

print(result1) # Output: 8

Example 2: Calculating exponentiation with modulus

result2 = pow(3, 4, 5)

print(result2) # Output: 1

Example 3: Calculating large exponentiation (power of 10)

result3 = pow(10, 100)

print(result3)

#Output:
10000000000000000000000000000000000000000000000000000000000000000000000000000000000000000000
00000000000000000000000000

Explanation of the Examples:

1. In Example 1, we use pow() to calculate the result of raising 2 to the power of 3. The function returns 8 as the result.

2. Example 2 demonstrates using pow() with modulus. We calculate 3 raised to the power of 4 modulo 5, which results in 1. This is equivalent to (3 * * 4) % 5.

3. In Example 3, we calculate a large exponentiation, raising 10 to the power of 100. The result is a very large number with 101 digits.

Tips:

- The pow() function is a convenient way to perform exponentiation operations, especially when dealing with large numbers or modular arithmetic.

- When using pow() with modulus, it calculates the result of raising the base to the specified exponent and then taking the remainder when divided by the modulus. This is useful in cryptographic and mathematical applications.

- If you need to calculate exponentiation without modulus, you can omit the third argument, as shown in Example 1.

- When working with very large numbers, be aware that the result of exponentiation can become extremely large and may not fit into the memory or may take a significant amount of time to compute.

- To calculate exponentiation with floating-point numbers, you can use the * * operator or the math.pow() function, which allows for non-integer exponents.

3.6 round()

Description:

The round() function in Python is used to round a floating-point number to a specified number of decimal places or to the nearest integer. It helps in controlling the precision of floating-point numbers and simplifying them for presentation or calculations.

Syntax:

round(number, ndigits=None)

- number: The floating-point number to be rounded.

- ndigits (optional): The number of decimal places to which number should be rounded. If not provided, it rounds to the nearest integer. (Default is None.)

Example of Usage:

 # Example 1: Rounding to the nearest integer

rounded_int = round(3.6)

print(rounded_int) # Output: 4

 # Example 2: Rounding to a specified number of decimal places

rounded_decimal = round(3.14159, 2)

print(rounded_decimal) # Output: 3.14

 # Example 3: Rounding to the nearest hundred

rounded_hundred = round(12345, -2)

print(rounded_hundred) # Output: 12300

Explanation of the Examples:

1. In Example 1, we use round() to round the floating-point number 3.6 to the nearest integer, which results in 4.

2. Example 2 demonstrates rounding the floating-point number 3.14159 to two decimal places. The result is 3.14, as it rounds to the nearest value with two decimal places.

3. In Example 3, we round the integer 12345 to the nearest hundred by specifying -2 as the ndigits argument. This rounds to the nearest multiple of 100, resulting in 12300.

Tips:

- The round() function is useful when you need to control the precision of floating-point numbers for display or calculations. It can help in avoiding excessive decimal places.

- When rounding to the nearest integer, you can omit the ndigits argument or provide None (default behavior). This will round to the nearest whole number.

- To round a number to a specific number of decimal places, pass the desired number of decimal places as the ndigits argument. For example, round(3.14159, 2) rounds to two decimal places.

- You can also round to positions to the left of the decimal point by specifying a negative value for ndigits. For instance, round(12345, -2) rounds to the nearest hundred.

- Be aware that rounding can introduce errors in some cases, especially when dealing with very large or very small floating-point numbers. Rounding behavior may also vary slightly due to the way floating-point arithmetic works.

- When performing financial calculations or other situations where precise decimal rounding is required, consider using the decimal module, which provides more control over decimal arithmetic.

3.7 sum()

Description:

The sum() function in Python is used to calculate the sum of all elements in an iterable, such as a list, tuple, or other iterable objects. It is a convenient way to find the total of all numeric values within a collection.

Syntax:

sum(iterable, start=0)

- iterable: The iterable from which you want to calculate the sum of elements.

- start (optional): The initial value of the sum. If not provided, it defaults to 0.

Example of Usage:

 # Example 1: Calculating the sum of a list of numbers

numbers = [1, 2, 3, 4, 5]

total = sum(numbers)

print(total) # Output: 15

Example 2: Calculating the sum of a tuple of numbers

values = (10, 20, 30, 40, 50)

total = sum(values)

print(total) # Output: 150

Example 3: Calculating the sum with a specified starting value

numbers = [1, 2, 3, 4, 5]

starting_value = 100

total = sum(numbers, starting_value)

print(total) # Output: 115

Explanation of the Examples:

1. In Example 1, we use sum() to calculate the sum of the numbers in a list (numbers). The function returns the total, which is 15.

2. Example 2 shows calculating the sum of numbers in a tuple (values). The total is 150, as it sums all the values.

3. In Example 3, we calculate the sum of numbers in a list (numbers) with a specified starting value of 100. The sum() function adds the numbers to the starting value, resulting in a total of 115.

Tips:

- The sum() function is particularly useful when you need to find the total of numerical values within an iterable. It simplifies the process of iterating through the elements and accumulating their sum.

- You can provide an optional starting value to the sum() function using the start parameter. This value is added to the sum of the elements in the iterable.

- The iterable can contain various numeric types, including integers, floats, and even complex numbers. sum() will handle these types correctly.

- Be cautious when using sum() with non-numeric data types or mixed types within the iterable, as it may not produce meaningful results or raise a TypeError. Ensure that the elements within the iterable are compatible for summation.

- If the iterable is empty, sum() returns the specified start value (default is 0). You can use this behavior to provide a default sum in such cases.

- When working with large datasets, consider the potential for integer overflow or floating-point precision issues, especially when summing a large number of elements. In such cases, alternative approaches may be necessary to handle very large values accurately.

3.8 math.ceil()

Description:

The math.ceil() function in Python is used to calculate the smallest integer greater than or equal to a given number (rounding up to the nearest whole number). It is commonly used when you need to ensure that a value is rounded up to the next integer, regardless of its fractional part.

Syntax:

import math

math.ceil(x)

- x: The number for which you want to calculate the ceiling value.

Example of Usage:

import math

 # Example 1: Rounding up a float to the nearest integer

value1 = 5.3

ceiling1 = math.ceil(value1)

print(ceiling1) # Output: 6

 # Example 2: Rounding up a negative float

value2 = -2.7

ceiling2 = math.ceil(value2)

print(ceiling2) # Output: -2 (remains unchanged since it's already greater than or equal to -2)

 # Example 3: Rounding up a positive integer (no change)

value3 = 10

ceiling3 = math.ceil(value3)

print(ceiling3) # Output: 10 (remains unchanged as it's already an integer)

Explanation of the Examples:

1. In Example 1, we use math.ceil() to round up the float 5.3 to the nearest integer, resulting in 6. This ensures that the value is always rounded up to the next whole number.

2. Example 2 demonstrates rounding up a negative float, -2.7. The math.ceil() function rounds it to -2, as -2 is the smallest integer that is greater than or equal to -2.7.

3. In Example 3, we provide a positive integer (10) as the input to math.ceil(). However, since it's already an integer, the function returns the same integer value, 10.

Tips:

- math.ceil() is particularly useful when you need to ensure that a value is rounded up to the nearest whole number, even if it has a fractional part. This is commonly used in various mathematical and engineering calculations.

- The math module must be imported before using math.ceil(), as shown in the syntax. You can import it using import math.

- When using math.ceil() with negative numbers, keep in mind that it rounds up toward positive infinity, which means that the result will be greater than or equal to the input value.

- If you want to round a value to the nearest integer (either up or down based on the fractional part), you can use the built-in round() function. math.ceil() always rounds up, while round() follows the standard rounding rules.

- Be aware that using math.ceil() with non-numeric or non-integer values may result in a TypeError. Ensure that the input is a numeric value before using this function.

3.9 math.floor()

Description:

The math.floor() function in Python is used to calculate the largest integer less than or equal to a given number (rounding down to the nearest whole number). It is commonly used when you need to ensure that a value is rounded down to the previous integer, regardless of its fractional part.

Syntax:

import math

math.floor(x)

- x: The number for which you want to calculate the floor value.

Example of Usage:

import math

 # Example 1: Rounding down a float to the nearest integer
value1 = 5.8

floor1 = math.floor(value1)

print(floor1) # Output: 5

Example 2: Rounding down a negative float

value2 = -2.7

floor2 = math.floor(value2)

print(floor2) # Output: -3 (rounded down to the nearest integer less than or equal to -2.7)

Example 3: Rounding down a positive integer (no change)

value3 = 10

floor3 = math.floor(value3)

print(floor3) # Output: 10 (remains unchanged as it's already an integer)

Explanation of the Examples:

1. In Example 1, we use math.floor() to round down the float 5.8 to the nearest integer, resulting in 5. This ensures that the value is always rounded down to the previous whole number.

2. Example 2 demonstrates rounding down a negative float, -2.7. The math.floor() function rounds it to -3, as -3 is the largest integer that is less than or equal to -2.7.

3. In Example 3, we provide a positive integer (10) as the input to math.floor(). However, since it's already an integer, the function returns the same integer value, 10.

Tips:

- math.floor() is particularly useful when you need to ensure that a value is rounded down to the nearest whole number, even if it has a fractional part. This is commonly used in various mathematical and engineering calculations.

- The math module must be imported before using math.floor(), as shown in the syntax. You can import it using import math.

- When using math.floor() with negative numbers, keep in mind that it rounds down toward negative infinity, which means that the result will be less than or equal to the input value.

- If you want to round a value to the nearest integer (either up or down based on the fractional part), you can use the built-in round() function. math.floor() always rounds down, while round() follows the standard rounding rules.

- Be aware that using math.floor() with non-numeric or non-integer values may result in a TypeError. Ensure that the input is a numeric value before using this function.

3.10 math.factorial()

Description:

The math.factorial() function in Python is used to calculate the factorial of a non-negative integer. The factorial of a non-negative integer n, denoted as n!, is the product of all positive integers from 1 to n. Factorials are often used in combinatorics, probability, and mathematical calculations.

Syntax:

import math

math.factorial(n)

- n: The non-negative integer for which you want to calculate the factorial.

Example of Usage:

import math

 # Example 1: Calculating the factorial of a non-negative integer

factorial1 = math.factorial(5) # Factorial of 5

print(factorial1) # Output: 120 (5! = 5 * 4 * 3 * 2 * 1 = 120)

 # Example 2: Calculating the factorial of 0 (0! = 1 by convention)

factorial2 = math.factorial(0)

print(factorial2) # Output: 1 (0! = 1)

 # Example 3: Calculating the factorial of a larger number

factorial3 = math.factorial(10) # Factorial of 10

print(factorial3) # Output: 3628800 (10! = 10 * 9 * 8 * 7 * 6 * 5 * 4 * 3 * 2 * 1 = 3628800)

Explanation of the Examples:

1. In Example 1, we use math.factorial() to calculate the factorial of 5, which is 120. This is because 5! is equal to 5 * 4 * 3 * 2 * 1 = 120.

2. Example 2 demonstrates calculating the factorial of 0. By convention, 0! is defined to be 1, so the function returns 1.

3. In Example 3, we calculate the factorial of a larger number, 10. The function returns 3628800 because 10! is equal to 10 * 9 * 8 * 7 * 6 * 5 * 4 * 3 * 2 * 1 = 3628800.

Tips:

- The math.factorial() function is used to calculate factorials of non-negative integers. It's commonly used in problems involving permutations, combinations, and counting arrangements.

- Factorials grow rapidly with increasing values of n. Be cautious when calculating factorials of large numbers, as they can become very large, potentially causing memory and performance issues.

- By convention, 0! is defined to be 1. This is because there is only one way to arrange zero items (no arrangement at all).

- The factorial function is used in probability calculations, such as calculating the number of permutations and combinations in statistics and combinatorics.

- Be aware that factorials of large numbers can exceed the representational limits of standard integer data types. In such cases, consider using libraries or techniques for handling arbitrary-precision arithmetic.

3.11 math.fsum()

Description:

The math.fsum() function in Python is used to calculate the accurate floating-point sum of a sequence of floating-point numbers. Unlike the built-in sum() function, which may accumulate rounding errors when summing a large number of floating-point values, math.fsum() provides a more precise result by using a higher precision floating-point arithmetic.

Syntax:

import math

math.fsum(iterable)

- iterable: An iterable (e.g., list, tuple, generator) containing floating-point numbers for which you want to calculate the sum.

Example of Usage:

import math

Example 1: Summing a list of floating-point numbers using math.fsum()

numbers = [0.1, 0.2, 0.3, 0.4, 0.5]

total = math.fsum(numbers)

print(total) # Output: 1.5 (accurate floating-point sum)

 # Example 2: Summing a large sequence of numbers with potential rounding errors

values = [0.1] * 10_000

total_builtin_sum = sum(values)

total_fsum = math.fsum(values)

print(total_builtin_sum) # Output: 1.0000000000000007 (rounding errors)

print(total_fsum) # Output: 1000.0 (accurate floating-point sum)

Explanation of the Examples:

1. In Example 1, we use math.fsum() to calculate the accurate sum of a list of floating-point numbers (numbers). The function returns 1.5 as the result, providing a precise floating-point sum.

2. Example 2 highlights the difference between using the built-in sum() function and math.fsum(). We create a list of 10,000 values, each set to 0.1, and calculate the sum using both methods. While the result of sum() accumulates rounding errors (1.0000000000000007), math.fsum() produces an accurate result of 1000.0.

Tips:

- Use math.fsum() when precision is important, especially when dealing with a large sequence of floating-point numbers where cumulative rounding errors can lead to inaccurate results.

- Be aware that math.fsum() may be slower than the built-in sum() for small lists or when speed is more critical than precision.

- Ensure that the input to math.fsum() is an iterable containing floating-point numbers. The function is designed to work with floating-point data.

- While math.fsum() provides higher precision than sum(), it still operates within the limits of floating-point arithmetic. Extreme values or very large datasets may still pose challenges, and alternative approaches, such as using the decimal module or other specialized libraries, may be necessary for maximum precision.

3.12 math.gcd()

Description:

The math.gcd() function in Python is used to calculate the greatest common divisor (GCD) of two or more integers. The GCD is the largest positive integer that divides each of the input integers without leaving a remainder. This function is useful in various mathematical and computational applications, such as reducing fractions to their simplest form.

Syntax:

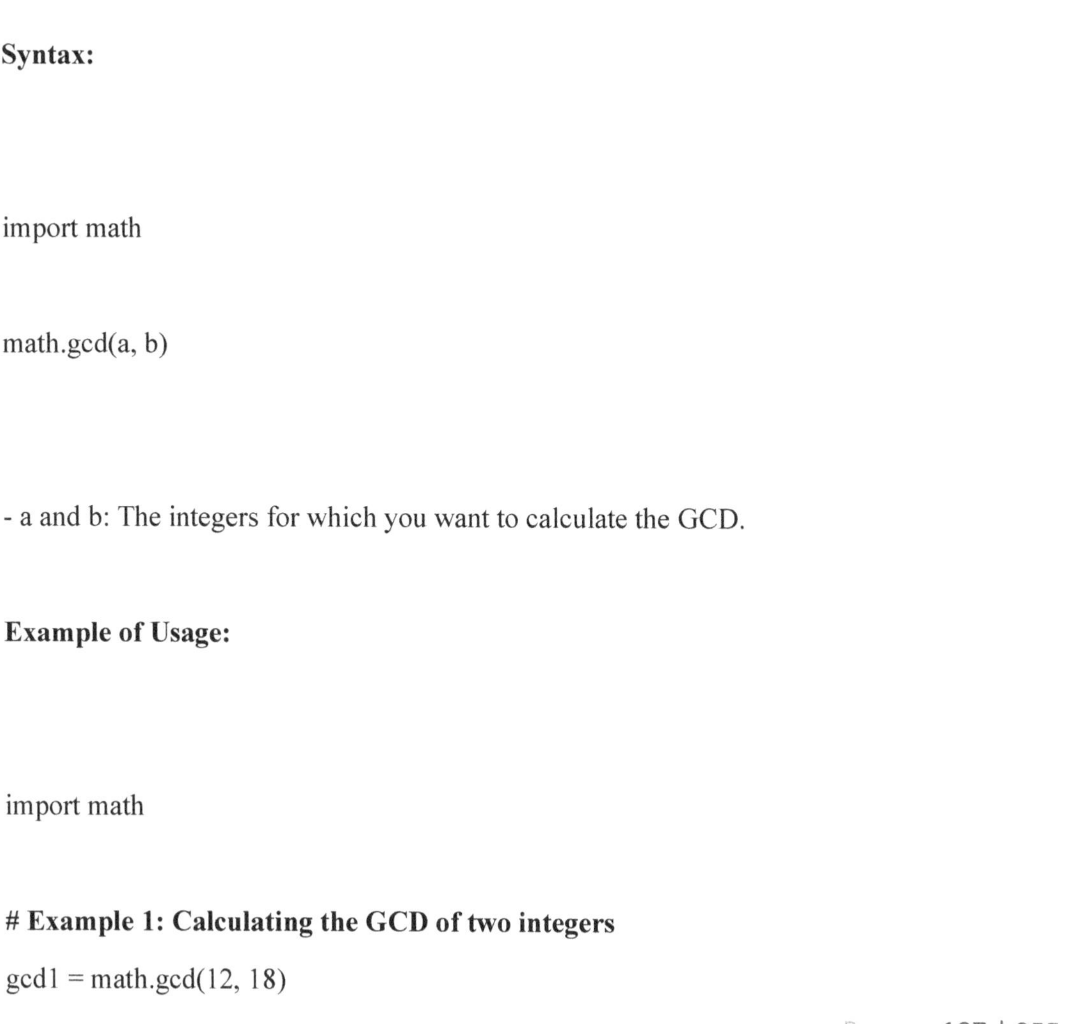

```python
import math
```

```python
math.gcd(a, b)
```

- a and b: The integers for which you want to calculate the GCD.

Example of Usage:

```python
import math
```

 # Example 1: Calculating the GCD of two integers

```python
gcd1 = math.gcd(12, 18)
```

print(gcd1) # Output: 6 (the largest integer that divides both 12 and 18 without remainder)

Example 2: Calculating the GCD of three integers

gcd2 = math.gcd(24, 36, 48)

print(gcd2) # Output: 12 (the largest integer that divides all three numbers without remainder)

Example 3: Calculating the GCD of negative integers

gcd3 = math.gcd(-36, 48)

print(gcd3) # Output: 12 (the GCD is positive even if input numbers are negative)

Explanation of the Examples:

1. In Example 1, we use math.gcd() to calculate the GCD of two integers, 12 and 18. The function returns 6 because 6 is the largest integer that divides both 12 and 18 without a remainder.

2. Example 2 demonstrates calculating the GCD of three integers, 24, 36, and 48. The function returns 12 as the GCD, which is the largest integer that divides all three numbers without leaving a remainder.

3. In Example 3, we calculate the GCD of two integers, -36 and 48. Even though one input is negative, the GCD is positive, and the function returns 12.

Tips:

- The math.gcd() function is useful for finding the GCD of two or more integers, which is often needed in mathematical computations and simplifying fractions.

- You can calculate the GCD of more than two integers by providing them as separate arguments to math.gcd(), as shown in Example 2.

- The GCD is always a non-negative integer, regardless of whether the input integers are positive or negative.

- Be cautious when using the GCD function with very large integers, as it may have performance implications. In such cases, consider alternative algorithms or libraries optimized for handling large numbers.

- If you need to calculate the GCD of a list of integers, you can use the functools.reduce() function in combination with math.gcd().

3.13 math.isqrt()

Description:

The math.isqrt() function in Python is used to calculate the integer square root of a non-negative integer. The integer square root is the largest integer whose square is less than or equal to the given non-negative integer. This function is useful when you need to find the largest integer value that, when squared, does not exceed a certain number.

Syntax:

import math

math.isqrt(n)

- n: The non-negative integer for which you want to calculate the integer square root.

Example of Usage:

import math

 # Example 1: Calculating the integer square root of a non-negative integer

sqrt1 = math.isqrt(16)

print(sqrt1) # Output: 4 (4^2 = 16)

 # Example 2: Calculating the integer square root of a larger non-negative integer

sqrt2 = math.isqrt(25)

print(sqrt2) # Output: 5 (5^2 = 25)

 # Example 3: Calculating the integer square root of a large non-negative integer

sqrt3 = math.isqrt(1234567890)

print(sqrt3) # Output: 35135 (35135^2 = 1234567225)

Explanation of the Examples:

1. In Example 1, we use math.isqrt() to calculate the integer square root of 16. The function returns 4 because 4 is the largest integer whose square (4^2) is less than or equal to 16.

2. Example 2 calculates the integer square root of 25, which is 5 because 5^2 equals 25.

3. In Example 3, we calculate the integer square root of the larger non-negative integer 1234567890. The function returns 35135 because 35135 is the largest integer whose square (35135^2) is less than or equal to 1234567890.

Tips:

- math.isqrt() is particularly useful when you need to find the integer value that, when squared, does not exceed a given number. It can be helpful in various mathematical and computational tasks.

- The input to math.isqrt() must be a non-negative integer. It will raise a ValueError if a negative value is provided.

- The result of math.isqrt() is always an integer, and it represents the largest integer whose square is less than or equal to the input value.

- If you need to calculate the square root of a non-integer or negative value, you can use the math.sqrt() function. However, keep in mind that math.sqrt() returns a floating-point result.

3.14 math.sqrt()

Description:

The math.sqrt() function in Python is used to calculate the square root of a non-negative number. It returns the positive square root of the given number. Square root is a mathematical operation that, when applied to a number, gives another number which, when multiplied by itself, equals the original number. This function is useful for various mathematical and scientific calculations.

Syntax:

import math

math.sqrt(x)

- x: The non-negative number for which you want to calculate the square root.

Example of Usage:

import math

 # Example 1: Calculating the square root of a non-negative number

sqrt1 = math.sqrt(25)

print(sqrt1) # Output: 5.0 (square root of 25 is 5)

 # Example 2: Calculating the square root of a decimal number

sqrt2 = math.sqrt(2.0)

print(sqrt2)   # Output: 1.4142135623730951 (square root of 2 is approximately 1.4142135623730951)

 # Example 3: Error when calculating the square root of a negative number

try:

   sqrt3 = math.sqrt(-9)

except ValueError as e:

   print(e) # Output: "math domain error" (square root of a negative number is undefined in real numbers)

Explanation of the Examples:

1. In Example 1, we use math.sqrt() to calculate the square root of the non-negative number 25. The function returns 5.0, which is the positive square root of 25.

2. Example 2 demonstrates calculating the square root of a decimal number, 2.0. The result is approximately 1.4142135623730951, which is the positive square root of 2.

3. In Example 3, we attempt to calculate the square root of a negative number, -9. This results in a ValueError because the square root of a negative number is undefined in the real number system.

Tips:

- math.sqrt() is commonly used when you need to find the positive square root of a non-negative number in mathematical and scientific computations.

- Be aware that attempting to calculate the square root of a negative number using math.sqrt() will result in a ValueError. If you need to calculate square roots of negative numbers, you should consider using complex numbers or other specialized mathematical techniques.

- The result of math.sqrt() is always a floating-point number, even if the input is an integer.

- Keep in mind that floating-point arithmetic may introduce small rounding errors when working with the square root of certain numbers. If precision is crucial, consider using the decimal module or other specialized libraries for arbitrary-precision arithmetic.

3.15 math.exp()

Description:

The math.exp() function in Python is used to calculate the exponential value of a given number. It returns the result of raising the mathematical constant e (approximately equal to 2.71828) to the power of the specified number. Exponential functions are common in various scientific and mathematical contexts.

Syntax:

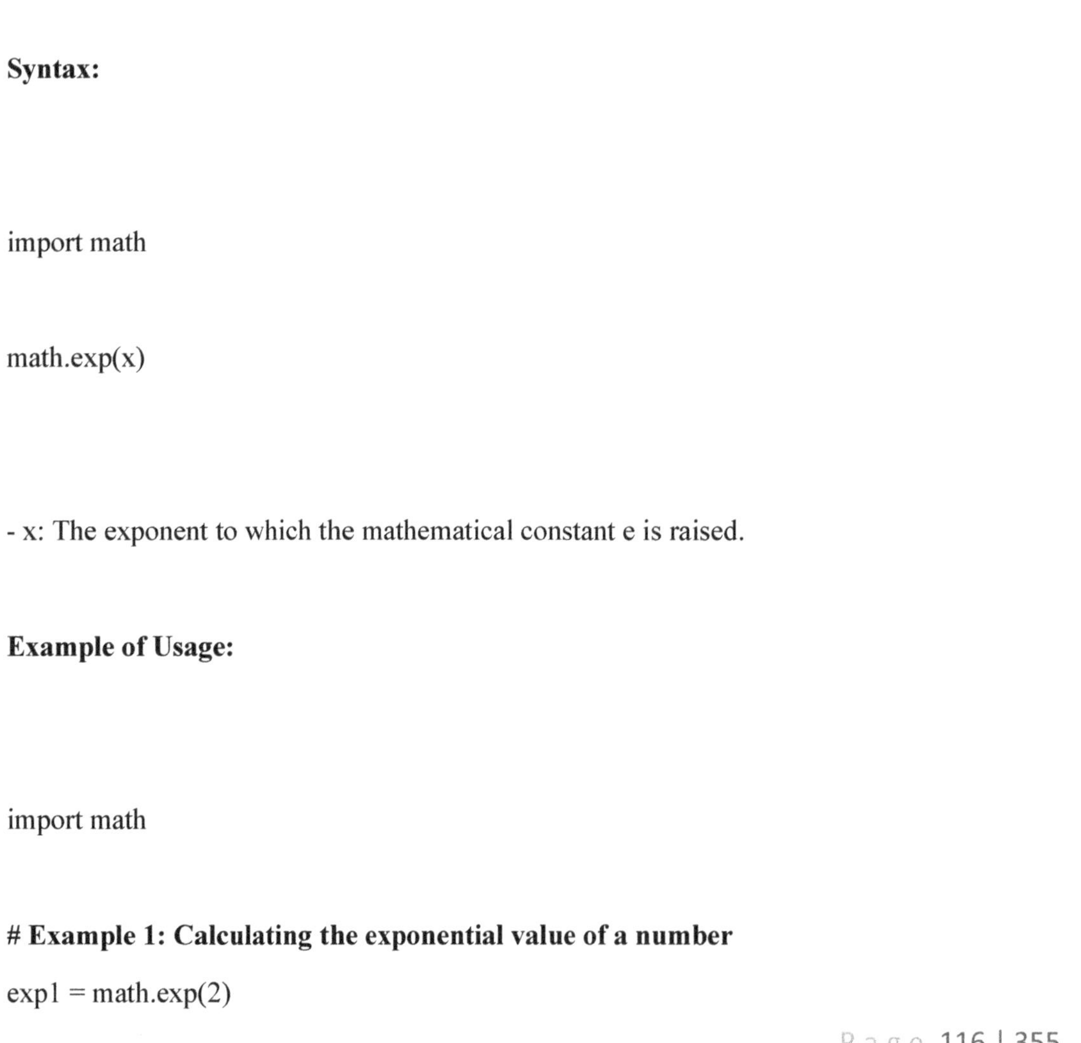

```python
import math
```

```python
math.exp(x)
```

- x: The exponent to which the mathematical constant e is raised.

Example of Usage:

```python
import math
```

 # Example 1: Calculating the exponential value of a number

```python
exp1 = math.exp(2)
```

print(exp1) # Output: 7.3890560989306495 (e^2 ≈ 7.3890560989306495)

Example 2: Calculating the exponential value of a negative number

exp2 = math.exp(-1)

print(exp2) # Output: 0.36787944117144233 (e^(-1) ≈ 0.36787944117144233)

Example 3: Calculating the exponential value of zero (e^0 = 1)

exp3 = math.exp(0)

print(exp3) # Output: 1.0 (e^0 = 1)

Explanation of the Examples:

1. In Example 1, we use math.exp() to calculate the exponential value of the number 2. The function returns approximately 7.3890560989306495, which is the result of raising e to the power of 2 (i.e., e^2).

2. Example 2 demonstrates calculating the exponential value of a negative number, -1. The result is approximately 0.36787944117144233, which is the result of raising e to the power of -1 (i.e., e^(-1)).

3. In Example 3, we calculate the exponential value of zero, which is 1. This is because e raised to the power of 0 is defined to be equal to 1 (i.e., e^0 = 1).

Tips:

- The math.exp() function is useful for calculating exponential values, which arise in various scientific and mathematical contexts, including calculus, probability, and growth models.

- Keep in mind that the result of math.exp() is always a floating-point number.

- Be aware that raising e to a large positive or negative exponent may result in very large or very small values, respectively, which can lead to numerical overflow or underflow. In such cases, you may need to handle these extreme values or use alternative techniques or libraries for numerical stability.

- If you need to calculate the natural logarithm (base e) of a number, you can use the math.log() function. The inverse operation of math.exp() is math.log().

3.16 math.log()

Description:

The math.log() function in Python is used to calculate the natural logarithm (base e) of a given number. It returns the result of the logarithm of the specified number with base e, where e is the mathematical constant approximately equal to 2.71828. Natural logarithms are common in mathematics, especially in calculus, and have various applications in scientific and engineering calculations.

Syntax:

import math

math.log(x)

- x: The number for which you want to calculate the natural logarithm.

Example of Usage:

import math

 # Example 1: Calculating the natural logarithm of a number

log1 = math.log(2.71828)

print(log1) # Output: 1.0 (ln(2.71828) = 1.0)

Example 2: Calculating the natural logarithm of a larger number

log2 = math.log(10)

print(log2) # Output: 2.302585092994046 (ln(10) ≈ 2.302585092994046)

Example 3: Calculating the natural logarithm of 1 (ln(1) = 0)

log3 = math.log(1)

print(log3) # Output: 0.0 (ln(1) = 0)

Explanation of the Examples:

1. In Example 1, we use math.log() to calculate the natural logarithm of the number 2.71828. The function returns 1.0, which is the result of taking the natural logarithm (ln) of 2.71828.

2. Example 2 demonstrates calculating the natural logarithm of a larger number, 10. The result is approximately 2.302585092994046, which is the natural logarithm of 10.

3. In Example 3, we calculate the natural logarithm of 1. The function returns 0.0 because the natural logarithm of 1 is defined to be 0.

Tips:

- The math.log() function is commonly used when you need to calculate natural logarithms in mathematical and scientific computations.

- Keep in mind that the result of math.log() is always a floating-point number.

- The natural logarithm has the property that ln(1) = 0. This property is often used in mathematical calculations.

- Be cautious when using logarithmic functions with values less than or equal to zero, as they are undefined for such values. You may need to handle special cases or use appropriate error handling when dealing with non-positive values.

- If you need to calculate logarithms with bases other than e, you can use the math.log() function in combination with a specified base. For example, to calculate the logarithm of a number with base 10, you can use math.log(x, 10).

3.17 math.log10()

Description:

The math.log10() function in Python is used to calculate the logarithm of a given number with base 10. It returns the result of taking the logarithm (base 10) of the specified number. Logarithms with base 10 are commonly used in various scientific and engineering calculations, especially when dealing with quantities measured on a logarithmic scale.

Syntax:

import math

math.log10(x)

- x: The number for which you want to calculate the base-10 logarithm.

Example of Usage:

import math

Example 1: Calculating the base-10 logarithm of a number

log10_1 = math.log10(100)

print(log10_1) # Output: 2.0 (log10(100) = 2.0)

Example 2: Calculating the base-10 logarithm of a non-integer

log10_2 = math.log10(3.1622776601683795)

print(log10_2) # Output: 0.5 (log10(3.1622776601683795) ≈ 0.5)

Example 3: Calculating the base-10 logarithm of 1 (log10(1) = 0)

log10_3 = math.log10(1)

print(log10_3) # Output: 0.0 (log10(1) = 0)

Explanation of the Examples:

1. In Example 1, we use math.log10() to calculate the base-10 logarithm of the number 100. The function returns 2.0, which is the result of taking the logarithm (base 10) of 100.

2. Example 2 demonstrates calculating the base-10 logarithm of a non-integer number, 3.1622776601683795. The result is approximately 0.5, which is the base-10 logarithm of 3.1622776601683795.

3. In Example 3, we calculate the base-10 logarithm of 1. The function returns 0.0 because the base-10 logarithm of 1 is defined to be 0.

Tips:

- The math.log10() function is commonly used when you need to calculate base-10 logarithms in mathematical and scientific computations, especially in fields like chemistry, biology, and geophysics where quantities are often measured on a logarithmic scale.

- The result of math.log10() is always a floating-point number.

- Be cautious when using logarithmic functions with values less than or equal to zero, as they are undefined for such values. You may need to handle special cases or use appropriate error handling when dealing with non-positive values.

- If you need to calculate logarithms with bases other than 10 or the natural logarithm (base e), you can use the math.log() function in combination with a specified base. For example, to calculate the logarithm of a number with base 2, you can use math.log(x, 2).

3.18 math.cos()

Description:

The math.cos() function in Python is used to calculate the cosine of an angle in radians. It returns the cosine value of the specified angle, which represents the ratio of the length of the adjacent side to the length of the hypotenuse in a right triangle. The math.cos() function is commonly used in trigonometry and geometry-related calculations.

Syntax:

import math

math.cos(x)

- x: The angle in radians for which you want to calculate the cosine.

Example of Usage:

import math

 # Example 1: Calculating the cosine of an angle in radians

cos1 = math.cos(math.pi) # Cosine of π (pi) radians

print(cos1) # Output: -1.0 (cos(π) = -1.0)

 # Example 2: Calculating the cosine of a specific angle in radians

angle_in_radians = math.radians(30) # Convert 30 degrees to radians

cos2 = math.cos(angle_in_radians) # Cosine of 30 degrees in radians

print(cos2) # Output: 0.86602540378 (cos(30 degrees) $\approx$ 0.86602540378)

 # Example 3: Calculating the cosine of 0 radians (cos(0) = 1)

cos3 = math.cos(0)

print(cos3) # Output: 1.0 (cos(0) = 1.0)

Explanation of the Examples:

1. In Example 1, we use math.cos() to calculate the cosine of π (pi) radians, which is -1.0. This is because the cosine of π radians is equal to -1.0.

2. Example 2 demonstrates calculating the cosine of a specific angle, 30 degrees, in radians. We first convert 30 degrees to radians using math.radians(), and then calculate the cosine of that angle, which is approximately 0.86602540378.

3. In Example 3, we calculate the cosine of 0 radians. The function returns 1.0 because the cosine of 0 radians is defined to be 1.0.

Tips:

```python
print(sin1)  # Output: 1.0 (sin(π/2) = 1.0)
```

Example 2: Calculating the sine of a specific angle in radians

```python
angle_in_radians = math.radians(45)  # Convert 45 degrees to radians

sin2 = math.sin(angle_in_radians)  # Sine of 45 degrees in radians

print(sin2)  # Output: 0.7071067811865475 (sin(45 degrees) ≈ 0.7071067811865475)
```

Example 3: Calculating the sine of 0 radians (sin(0) = 0)

```python
sin3 = math.sin(0)

print(sin3)  # Output: 0.0 (sin(0) = 0.0)
```

Explanation of the Examples:

1. In Example 1, we use math.sin() to calculate the sine of $\pi/2$ radians, which is 1.0. This is because the sine of $\pi/2$ radians is equal to 1.0.

2. Example 2 demonstrates calculating the sine of a specific angle, 45 degrees, in radians. We first convert 45 degrees to radians using math.radians(), and then calculate the sine of that angle, which is approximately 0.7071067811865475.

3. In Example 3, we calculate the sine of 0 radians. The function returns 0.0 because the sine of 0 radians is defined to be 0.0.

Tips:

3.20 math.tan()

Description:

The math.tan() function in Python is used to calculate the tangent of an angle in radians. It returns the tangent value of the specified angle, which represents the ratio of the length of the opposite side to the length of the adjacent side in a right triangle. The math.tan() function is commonly used in trigonometry and geometry-related calculations.

Syntax:

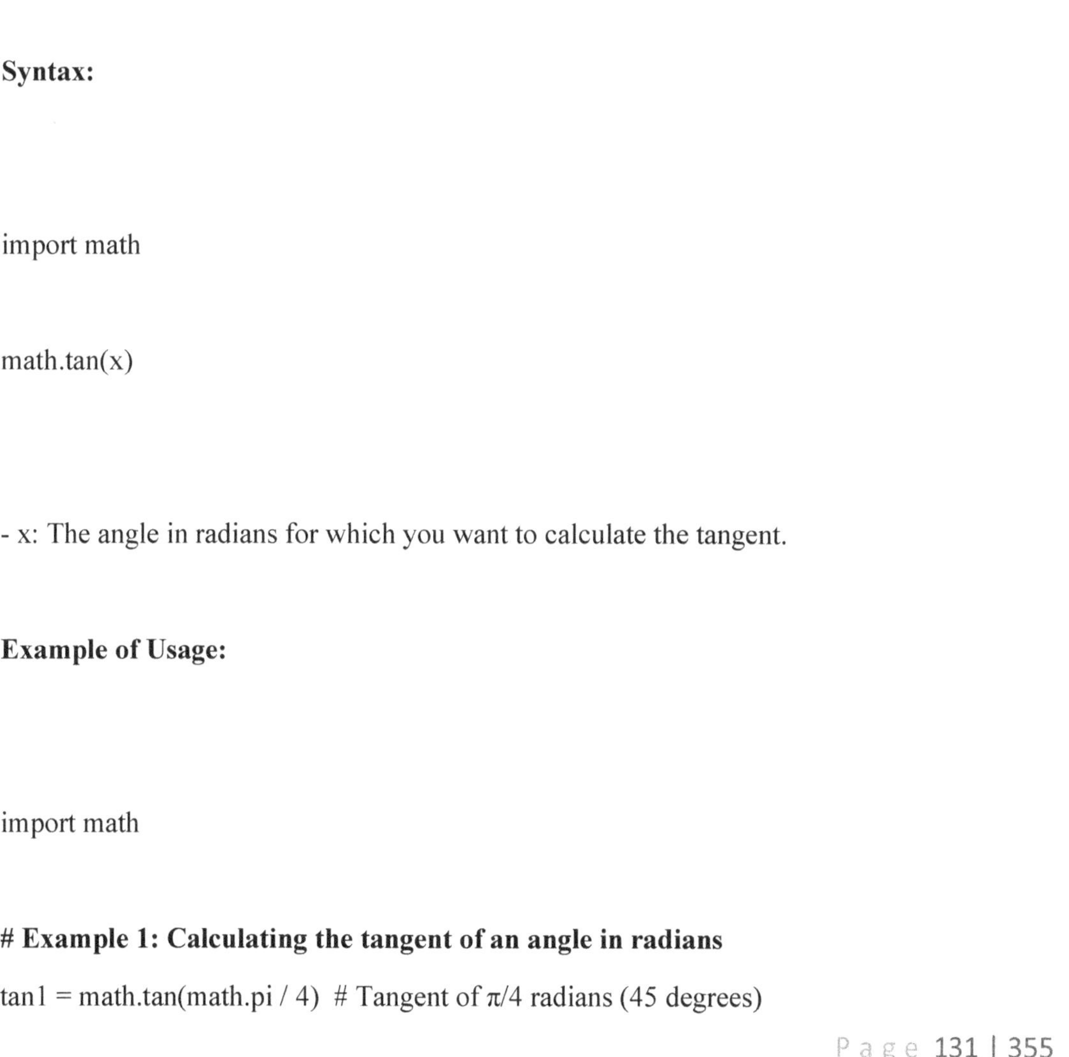

```python
import math

math.tan(x)
```

- x: The angle in radians for which you want to calculate the tangent.

Example of Usage:

```python
import math
```

 # Example 1: Calculating the tangent of an angle in radians

```python
tan1 = math.tan(math.pi / 4)  # Tangent of π/4 radians (45 degrees)
```

print(tan1) # Output: 1.0 (tan(π/4) = 1.0)

 # Example 2: Calculating the tangent of a specific angle in radians

angle_in_radians = math.radians(60) # Convert 60 degrees to radians

tan2 = math.tan(angle_in_radians) # Tangent of 60 degrees in radians

print(tan2) # Output: 1.7320508075688772 (tan(60 degrees) ≈ 1.7320508075688772)

 # Example 3: Calculating the tangent of 0 radians (tan(0) = 0)

tan3 = math.tan(0)

print(tan3) # Output: 0.0 (tan(0) = 0.0)

Explanation of the Examples:

1. In Example 1, we use math.tan() to calculate the tangent of π/4 radians (which is equivalent to 45 degrees). The function returns 1.0, which is the result of taking the tangent of π/4 radians.

2. Example 2 demonstrates calculating the tangent of a specific angle, 60 degrees, in radians. We first convert 60 degrees to radians using math.radians(), and then calculate the tangent of that angle, which is approximately 1.7320508075688772.

3. In Example 3, we calculate the tangent of 0 radians. The function returns 0.0 because the tangent of 0 radians is defined to be 0.0.

Tips:

- The math.tan() function is a fundamental trigonometric function and is used in various fields, including physics, engineering, computer graphics, and navigation.

- Make sure to provide the angle in radians as the argument to math.tan(). If you have an angle in degrees, you can use math.radians() to convert it to radians before calculating the tangent.

- Be cautious when calculating the tangent of angles close to multiples of $\pi/2$ radians (90 degrees), as the tangent becomes undefined for such angles. You may encounter large values or mathematical errors in such cases.

- The tangent function has a periodic behavior with a period of π radians (approximately 3.14159265 radians), so tan(x) is equal to tan(x + π) for any real number x.

IV.
Iterable Functions

4.1 all()

Description:

The all() function in Python is used to determine whether all elements in an iterable (such as a list, tuple, or other iterable object) evaluate to True. It returns True if all elements are considered "truthy," and False otherwise. If the iterable is empty, the all() function also returns True by default.

Syntax:

all(iterable)

- iterable: An iterable object (e.g., a list, tuple, or generator) containing the elements to be checked.

Example of Usage:

Example 1: Using all() with a list

list1 = [True, True, False, True]

result1 = all(list1)

print(result1) # Output: False (Not all elements are True)

Example 2: Using all() with an empty list (returns True by default)

empty_list = []

result2 = all(empty_list)

print(result2) # Output: True (All elements (none) are considered True in an empty list)

Example 3: Using all() with a tuple

tuple1 = (10, 20, 30, 40)

result3 = all(tuple1)

print(result3) # Output: True (All elements are considered True)

Example 4: Using all() with a generator expression

numbers = (x % 2 == 0 for x in range(1, 6)) # Generator expression to check if numbers are even

result4 = all(numbers)

print(result4) # Output: False (Not all numbers are even)

Explanation of the Examples:

1. In Example 1, we use all() with a list list1, which contains a mix of True and False values. The function returns False because not all elements in the list are True.

2. Example 2 demonstrates using all() with an empty list empty_list. In this case, the function returns True because there are no elements in the list, and an empty iterable is considered to have all elements as True.

3. In Example 3, we use all() with a tuple tuple1, which contains only numeric values. Since all elements in the tuple are considered "truthy," the function returns True.

4. Example 4 uses all() with a generator expression to check if a sequence of numbers from 1 to 5 is even. The generator expression evaluates to (False, True, False, True, False), and the function returns False because not all numbers in the sequence are even.

Tips:

- The all() function is often used when you need to check if all elements in an iterable satisfy a specific condition or are considered "truthy."

- An empty iterable (e.g., an empty list or tuple) is considered to have all elements as True, so all([]) will return True by default.

- You can use the any() function to check if at least one element in an iterable evaluates to True.

4.2 any()

Description:

The any() function in Python is used to determine whether at least one element in an iterable (such as a list, tuple, or other iterable object) evaluates to True. It returns True if any element is considered "truthy," and False if all elements are "falsy." If the iterable is empty, the any() function returns False by default.

Syntax:

any(iterable)

- iterable: An iterable object (e.g., a list, tuple, or generator) containing the elements to be checked.

Example of Usage:

 # Example 1: Using any() with a list

list1 = [False, False, True, False]

result1 = any(list1)

print(result1) # Output: True (At least one element is True)

Example 2: Using any() with an empty list (returns False by default)

empty_list = []

result2 = any(empty_list)

print(result2) # Output: False (There are no elements in the list)

Example 3: Using any() with a tuple

tuple1 = (0, 0, 0, 42)

result3 = any(tuple1)

print(result3) # Output: True (At least one element is considered True)

Example 4: Using any() with a generator expression

numbers = (x % 2 == 0 for x in range(1, 6)) # Generator expression to check if numbers are even

result4 = any(numbers)

print(result4) # Output: True (At least one number is even)

Explanation of the Examples:

1. In Example 1, we use any() with a list list1, which contains a mix of True and False values. The function returns True because at least one element in the list is True.

2. Example 2 demonstrates using any() with an empty list empty_list. In this case, the function returns False because there are no elements in the list, and an empty iterable is considered to have no elements that are True.

3. In Example 3, we use any() with a tuple tuple1, which contains both 0 (considered "falsy") and 42 (considered "truthy"). The function returns True because at least one element in the tuple is considered "truthy."

4. Example 4 uses any() with a generator expression to check if a sequence of numbers from 1 to 5 is even. The generator expression evaluates to (False, True, False, True, False), and the function returns True because at least one number in the sequence is even.

Tips:

- The any() function is often used when you need to check if at least one element in an iterable satisfies a specific condition or is considered "truthy."

- An empty iterable (e.g., an empty list or tuple) is considered to have no elements that are True, so any([]) will return False by default.

- You can use the all() function to check if all elements in an iterable evaluate to True.

4.3 enumerate()

Description:

The enumerate() function in Python is used to iterate over an iterable (e.g., a list, tuple, or string) while keeping track of the index or position of each element. It returns an iterator that generates pairs of index and value for each element in the iterable. This is particularly useful when you need both the value and its position in the iterable during iteration.

Syntax:

enumerate(iterable, start=0)

- iterable: The iterable object (e.g., a list, tuple, or string) that you want to iterate over.

- start (optional): The index to start counting from. By default, it is 0.

Example of Usage:

 # Example 1: Using enumerate() with a list

fruits = ["apple", "banana", "cherry"]

enumerated_fruits = list(enumerate(fruits))

print(enumerated_fruits)

Output: [(0, 'apple'), (1, 'banana'), (2, 'cherry')]

 # Example 2: Using enumerate() with a starting index

colors = ["red", "green", "blue"]

enumerated_colors = list(enumerate(colors, start=1))

print(enumerated_colors)

Output: [(1, 'red'), (2, 'green'), (3, 'blue')]

 # Example 3: Using enumerate() with a string

word = "Python"

enumerated_word = list(enumerate(word))

print(enumerated_word)

Output: [(0, 'P'), (1, 'y'), (2, 't'), (3, 'h'), (4, 'o'), (5, 'n')]

Explanation of the Examples:

1. In Example 1, we use enumerate() with a list of fruits. The function returns an iterator that generates pairs of index and value for each fruit in the list. We convert the iterator to a list to display the results.

2. Example 2 demonstrates using enumerate() with a starting index (start=1). The function assigns indices starting from 1 and generates pairs for colors in the list.

3. In Example 3, we use enumerate() with a string (word). The function generates pairs of index and character for each character in the string.

Tips:

- The enumerate() function is useful when you want to iterate over elements in an iterable and need to know the position or index of each element.

- By default, the counting starts from 0, but you can specify a different starting index using the start parameter.

- The result of enumerate() is an iterator, so you often convert it to a list or another iterable type (e.g., tuple) if you want to work with the enumerated values.

- You can use destructuring (tuple unpacking) to separate the index and value in a more concise way during iteration, e.g., for index, value in enumerate(iterable).

- enumerate() is commonly used in for loops when you need both the value and the index of each element.

4.4 filter()

Description:

The filter() function in Python is used to filter elements from an iterable (e.g., a list, tuple, or other iterable object) based on a specified condition. It returns an iterator that generates elements from the iterable for which the given condition evaluates to True. Essentially, it allows you to create a new iterable containing only the elements that meet the specified criteria.

Syntax:

filter(function, iterable)

- function: A function that defines the condition to filter elements. It should return True or False for each element in the iterable.

- iterable: The iterable object containing the elements to be filtered.

Example of Usage:

 # Example 1: Using filter() to filter even numbers from a list

numbers = [1, 2, 3, 4, 5, 6]

filtered_numbers = list(filter(lambda x: x % 2 == 0, numbers))

print(filtered_numbers)

Output: [2, 4, 6]

 # Example 2: Using filter() to filter names starting with 'A' from a list

names = ["Alice", "Bob", "Anna", "David", "Alex"]

filtered_names = list(filter(lambda name: name.startswith("A"), names))

print(filtered_names)

Output: ['Alice', 'Anna', 'Alex']

Explanation of the Examples:

1. In Example 1, we use filter() to filter even numbers from a list of numbers. We provide a lambda function that checks whether a number is even (returns True if the number modulo 2 is 0). The result is a new list containing only the even numbers.

2. Example 2 demonstrates using filter() to filter names starting with the letter 'A' from a list of names. The lambda function checks whether each name starts with 'A'. The result is a new list containing only the names that satisfy the condition.

Tips:

- The filter() function is often used when you want to select specific elements from an iterable based on a custom condition.

- You can use a lambda function, a regular function, or other callable objects as the condition in the filter() function.

- The result of filter() is an iterator, so you often convert it to a list or another iterable type (e.g., tuple) if you want to work with the filtered values.

- If you're working with complex conditions, consider using a named function instead of a lambda function for better readability.

- You can filter elements based on various conditions, such as checking for equality, greater than or less than comparisons, or more complex criteria.

- Keep in mind that the filtered iterable may have fewer elements than the original iterable, depending on the condition you provide.

4.5 len()

Description:

The len() function in Python is used to determine the number of elements in an iterable, such as a list, tuple, string, or other iterable objects. It returns the length or the count of items in the given iterable.

Syntax:

len(iterable)

- iterable: The iterable object for which you want to find the length.

Example of Usage:

 # Example 1: Using len() with a list

fruits = ["apple", "banana", "cherry"]

length_of_fruits = len(fruits)

print(length_of_fruits)

Output: 3

Example 2: Using len() with a string

word = "Python"

length_of_word = len(word)

print(length_of_word)

Output: 6

Example 3: Using len() with a tuple

numbers = (1, 2, 3, 4, 5)

length_of_numbers = len(numbers)

print(length_of_numbers)

Output: 5

Explanation of the Examples:

1. In Example 1, we use len() with a list fruits to find the number of elements in the list. The function returns 3 because there are three items in the list.

2. Example 2 demonstrates using len() with a string word. The function returns 6 because the string contains six characters.

3. In Example 3, we use len() with a tuple numbers. The function returns 5 because there are five elements in the tuple.

Tips:

- The len() function is a built-in function in Python and is commonly used to determine the size or length of various iterable objects.

- It is important to note that len() counts the number of items or elements in the iterable, so for a string, it counts individual characters, and for a list or tuple, it counts the number of elements.

- You can use the result of len() in various programming tasks, such as creating loops, checking if an iterable is empty, or comparing the sizes of different iterables.

- Be cautious when using len() with objects that do not support it. For instance, you cannot use len() with a numeric value or a dictionary. It is primarily meant for iterable objects.

4.6 map()

Description:

The map() function in Python is used to apply a given function to each item in an iterable (e.g., a list, tuple, or other iterable object) and return an iterator that yields the results of applying the function to each element. It allows you to perform an operation on each element of the iterable and collect the results in a new iterable.

Syntax:

map(function, iterable, ...)

- function: A function that defines the operation to be applied to each element in the iterable.

- iterable: The iterable object containing the elements to be processed.

- ... (optional): Additional iterables, if multiple iterables are to be processed together. The function should take as many arguments as there are iterables.

Example of Usage:

 # Example 1: Using map() to square each number in a list

numbers = [1, 2, 3, 4, 5]

squared_numbers = list(map(lambda x: x 2, numbers))

print(squared_numbers)

Output: [1, 4, 9, 16, 25]

 # Example 2: Using map() to concatenate corresponding elements from two lists

names = ["Alice", "Bob", "Charlie"]

surnames = ["Smith", "Johnson", "Brown"]

full_names = list(map(lambda x, y: x + " " + y, names, surnames))

print(full_names)

Output: ['Alice Smith', 'Bob Johnson', 'Charlie Brown']

Explanation of the Examples:

1. In Example 1, we use map() to square each number in a list numbers. The lambda function lambda x: x 2 is applied to each element in the list, resulting in a new list containing the squared values.

2. Example 2 demonstrates using map() to concatenate corresponding elements from two lists names and surnames. The lambda function lambda x, y: x + " " + y takes two arguments and combines them to create a full name. The function is applied element-wise to both lists, resulting in a new list of full names.

Tips:

- The map() function is useful when you need to apply a specific operation or function to each element in an iterable and collect the results in a new iterable.

- You can use both built-in functions and custom functions as the function argument in map(). In the examples, we used lambda functions for simplicity.

- If you need to apply a function to multiple iterables simultaneously, provide multiple iterables as arguments to map(), and ensure that the provided function can accept as many arguments as there are iterables.

- The result of map() is an iterator, so you often convert it to a list or another iterable type (e.g., tuple) if you want to work with the mapped values.

- Keep in mind that map() is a lazy operation, meaning it doesn't compute the values until they are requested. If you need to compute and store the mapped values immediately, convert the result to a list or another appropriate data structure.

- Consider using list comprehensions as an alternative to map() when the operation is simple and doesn't require a separate function. List comprehensions are often more readable for such cases.

Description:

The next() function in Python is used to retrieve the next item from an iterable (e.g., an iterator) and advance the iterator's position. It allows you to access elements from an iterable one by one. When there are no more items to retrieve, the next() function raises the StopIteration exception or returns a default value if a second argument is provided.

Syntax:

next(iterator, default)

- iterator: The iterator from which to retrieve the next item.

- default (optional): A value to return if there are no more items in the iterator. If not provided, the function raises StopIteration when the iterator is exhausted.

Example of Usage:

 # Example 1: Using next() to retrieve items from an iterator

numbers = [1, 2, 3, 4, 5]

iterator = iter(numbers)

Retrieve items one by one

```python
item1 = next(iterator)
print(item1)  # Output: 1


item2 = next(iterator)
print(item2)  # Output: 2


item3 = next(iterator)
print(item3)  # Output: 3
```

 # Example 2: Using next() with a default value

```python
iterator = iter([])  # An empty list
item = next(iterator, "No more items")
print(item)  # Output: "No more items"
```

Explanation of the Examples:

1. In Example 1, we use next() to retrieve items from an iterator created from a list numbers. The iter() function is used to obtain an iterator from the list. We call next(iterator) multiple times to access each item in the list one by one.

2. Example 2 demonstrates using next() with a default value. In this case, we create an iterator from an empty list and use next(iterator, "No more items"). Since the iterator is empty, it returns the default value "No more items".

Tips:

- The next() function is commonly used when iterating over custom objects or when you need to retrieve items from an iterable one at a time.

- If you don't provide a default value and there are no more items in the iterator, the next() function raises the StopIteration exception. You can catch this exception to handle the end of iteration gracefully.

- It's important to ensure that you don't call next() when the iterator is exhausted (i.e., there are no more items) without providing a default value or handling the StopIteration exception.

- You can use next() to iterate over items in an iterable conditionally, allowing you to skip or process items based on specific criteria.

- When working with custom iterators or objects, you can implement the __next__() method to define the behavior of the next() function for your objects. This allows you to create custom iteration logic.

4.8 reversed()

Description:

The reversed() function in Python is used to reverse the elements of an iterable object, such as a list, tuple, or string. It returns a reverse iterator that allows you to iterate over the elements in the reverse order, starting from the last element and moving towards the first element.

Syntax:

reversed(iterable)

- iterable: The iterable object whose elements you want to reverse.

Example of Usage:

 # Example 1: Using reversed() with a list

numbers = [1, 2, 3, 4, 5]

reversed_numbers = list(reversed(numbers))

print(reversed_numbers)

Output: [5, 4, 3, 2, 1]

 # Example 2: Using reversed() with a string

word = "Python"

reversed_word = "".join(reversed(word))

print(reversed_word)

Output: "nohtyP"

Explanation of the Examples:

1. In Example 1, we use reversed() with a list numbers to reverse the order of its elements. We convert the result to a list using list() to see the reversed list.

2. Example 2 demonstrates using reversed() with a string word. We use " ".join() to join the reversed characters back into a string. This effectively reverses the string.

Tips:

- The reversed() function is particularly useful when you need to iterate over elements in reverse order without modifying the original iterable.

- Keep in mind that the result of reversed() is a reverse iterator, which means you can use it in a for loop to iterate over elements in reverse order.

- You can use reversed() with any iterable, including lists, tuples, strings, and more.

- If you only need to reverse a list in-place (i.e., modify the original list), you can use the list.reverse() method for lists.

- For strings, you can use slicing with a step of -1 ([::-1]) to achieve the same result as reversed(). However, reversed() may be more convenient when working with other iterable types.

- While reversed() is useful for simple reversing of iterables, it does not modify the original iterable. If you need to permanently reverse a list, you can assign the result of reversed() back to the original variable, or you can use slicing to modify the list in-place.

4.9 slice()

Description:

The slice() function in Python is used to create a slice object that defines a range of indices for slicing an iterable (e.g., a list, tuple, or string). Slice objects are often used with sequences to extract a portion of the sequence, such as a sub-list or a substring.

Syntax:

slice(start, stop, step)

- start (optional): The starting index of the slice (inclusive). If not provided, it defaults to None, indicating the beginning of the iterable.

- stop (optional): The ending index of the slice (exclusive). If not provided, it defaults to None, indicating the end of the iterable.

- step (optional): The step or stride for selecting elements. If not provided, it defaults to None, indicating a step of 1.

Example of Usage:

 # Example 1: Using slice() with a list

numbers = [0, 1, 2, 3, 4, 5, 6, 7, 8, 9]

```python
# Create a slice object
my_slice = slice(2, 7, 2)


# Use the slice object to extract elements from the list
result = numbers[my_slice]
print(result)
# Output: [2, 4, 6]
```

Example 2: Using slice() with a string

```python
text = "Python Programming"


# Create a slice object
my_slice = slice(7, 18)


# Use the slice object to extract a substring
substring = text[my_slice]
print(substring)
# Output: "Programming"
```

Explanation of the Examples:

1. In Example 1, we create a slice object my_slice with a start index of 2, an end index of 7, and a step of 2. We then use this slice object to extract elements from the list numbers. The result is a new list containing the elements [2, 4, 6].

2. Example 2 demonstrates using slice() with a string text. We create a slice object my_slice with a start index of 7 and an end index of 18. This slice object is used to extract a substring from the original string, resulting in the string "Programming".

Tips:

- Slice objects are useful for defining slices with specific start, end, and step values, especially when you want to reuse the same slice configuration multiple times.

- When you create a slice object, you can omit any of the three parameters (start, stop, and step). The omitted parameters are treated as None, which indicates the default behavior (beginning, end, or step of 1, respectively).

- You can use slice objects in indexing to extract portions of an iterable. For example, numbers[my_slice] extracts elements from the list numbers based on the slice object my_slice.

- Slice objects are commonly used with strings, lists, tuples, and other iterable types. They allow you to easily create sublists, substrings, and sub-sequences.

- Be cautious when specifying slice indices to ensure that you do not exceed the boundaries of the iterable. IndexError can occur if the indices are out of range.

4.10 sorted()

Description:

The sorted() function in Python is used to return a sorted version of an iterable (e.g., a list, tuple, or string). It can sort elements in ascending or descending order, and it can be applied to a wide range of iterable types. The original iterable remains unchanged, and the sorted version is returned as a new iterable.

Syntax:

sorted(iterable, key=None, reverse=False)

- iterable: The iterable to be sorted.

- key (optional): A function that is applied to each element to determine the sorting key. The elements are sorted based on the values returned by this function. If not provided, the elements are sorted based on their natural order.

- reverse (optional): A boolean value that determines the sorting order. If True, the elements are sorted in descending order; if False (the default), they are sorted in ascending order.

Example of Usage:

 # Example 1: Sorting a list of numbers in ascending order

numbers = [5, 2, 8, 1, 9]

sorted_numbers = sorted(numbers)

print(sorted_numbers)

Output: [1, 2, 5, 8, 9]

 # Example 2: Sorting a list of strings in descending order by length

fruits = ["banana", "apple", "cherry", "date"]

sorted_fruits = sorted(fruits, key=len, reverse=True)

print(sorted_fruits)

Output: ['banana', 'cherry', 'apple', 'date']

Explanation of the Examples:

1. In Example 1, we use sorted() to sort a list of numbers numbers in ascending order. Since no key or reverse parameters are provided, the elements are sorted based on their natural order (ascending).

2. Example 2 demonstrates sorting a list of strings fruits in descending order by their lengths. We use the len function as the key to determine the sorting key, and reverse=True is specified to sort in descending order.

Tips:

- The sorted() function returns a new iterable containing the sorted elements. It does not modify the original iterable.

- If you want to sort a list in-place (i.e., modify the original list), you can use the list.sort() method for lists.

- The key parameter allows you to specify a custom function that calculates a sorting key for each element. This is useful when you want to sort based on specific criteria, such as sorting strings by length or sorting custom objects based on a particular attribute.

- To sort elements in descending order, set reverse=True. By default, the elements are sorted in ascending order.

- The sorted() function is versatile and can be used with various iterable types, including lists, tuples, strings, and more.

- If you want to sort elements based on multiple criteria, you can use a custom sorting key function that returns a tuple of values to be used as the sorting key.

- You can also use the sorted() function with custom comparison functions using the key parameter, allowing you to define complex sorting logic.

Description:

The zip() function in Python is used to combine multiple iterables (e.g., lists, tuples) into an iterator that generates tuples containing elements from the input iterables. It pairs elements from each iterable at the same index, creating a new iterable of tuples. The resulting iterator stops when the shortest input iterable is exhausted.

Syntax:

zip(iterable1, iterable2, ...)

- iterable1, iterable2, ... (at least one iterable): The iterables to be combined. You can provide multiple iterables separated by commas.

Example of Usage:

 # Example 1: Combining two lists into tuples

names = ["Alice", "Bob", "Charlie"]

scores = [85, 92, 78]

Use zip() to pair elements from the two lists

name_score_pairs = zip(names, scores)

Convert the zip object to a list of tuples

pairs_list = list(name_score_pairs)

print(pairs_list)

Output: [('Alice', 85), ('Bob', 92), ('Charlie', 78)]

 # Example 2: Using zip() with three lists

items = ["apple", "banana", "cherry"]

prices = [1.0, 0.5, 1.5]

quantities = [3, 5, 2]

Combine three lists into tuples using zip()

shopping_cart = zip(items, prices, quantities)

Convert the zip object to a list of tuples

cart_list = list(shopping_cart)

print(cart_list)

Output: [('apple', 1.0, 3), ('banana', 0.5, 5), ('cherry', 1.5, 2)]

Explanation of the Examples:

1. In Example 1, we have two lists, names and scores, representing names and corresponding scores. We use the zip() function to pair elements from these lists into tuples, creating a new iterable of tuples. The resulting list of tuples contains pairs of names and scores.

2. Example 2 demonstrates the use of zip() with three lists: items, prices, and quantities. We use zip() to combine these lists into tuples, creating a shopping cart representation where each tuple contains an item name, its price, and quantity.

Tips:

- zip() is particularly useful when you need to work with multiple iterables simultaneously and maintain a one-to-one correspondence between their elements.

- The resulting iterable from zip() can be converted to other data structures, such as lists or tuples, using list(), tuple(), or other constructor functions.

- If the input iterables are of unequal lengths, zip() will stop creating pairs when the shortest iterable is exhausted. Any remaining elements in the longer iterables will be ignored.

- You can use zip() with any iterable type, including lists, tuples, strings, and more.

- When working with dictionaries, you can use zip() to combine keys and values. For example, dict(zip(keys, values)) creates a dictionary from two lists, where the keys are taken from one list and the values from another.

- If you need to unzip (i.e., separate) the pairs created by zip(), you can use the zip() function again or the * unpacking operator. For example, names, scores = zip(*pairs_list) will separate the names and scores back into two separate iterables.

V. Evaluating Functions

5.1 callable()

Description:

The callable() function in Python is used to determine if an object can be called as a function. It checks whether the object is a callable function, method, or any other callable object that can be invoked using the function call syntax (()) with arguments. If the object is callable, callable() returns True; otherwise, it returns False.

Syntax:

callable(object)

- object: The object to be checked for callability.

Example of Usage:

 # Example 1: Check if a function is callable

```python
def greet(name):

    print(f"Hello, {name}!")


print(callable(greet))  # Output: True
```

 # Example 2: Check if a non-function object is callable

```python
class MyClass:

    def my_method(self):

        print("This is a method.")


obj = MyClass()
print(callable(obj))  # Output: True
```

 # Example 3: Check if a non-callable object is callable

```python
number = 42

print(callable(number))  # Output: False
```

Explanation of the Examples:

1. In Example 1, we define a function greet() and use callable() to check if it is callable. Since greet is a function, callable(greet) returns True.

2. Example 2 demonstrates checking the callability of a method within a class. We create an instance of MyClass and check if the my_method() is callable. It returns True since methods are callable.

3. Example 3 checks the callability of a non-callable object (number). In this case, callable(number) returns False.

Tips:

- callable() can be helpful when you want to determine if an object can be called as a function before attempting to call it. This can be useful for handling different types of objects gracefully in your code.

- Common objects that are callable include functions, methods, classes, and callable objects created with the __call__ method.

- Objects like numbers, strings, and most built-in types are not callable and will return False when checked with callable().

- When using callable(), make sure to pass the object you want to check as an argument to the function.

- Be aware that defining a callable object doesn't necessarily mean the object will behave as expected when called. Always consider the intended behavior of the object before invoking it as a function.

5.2 classmethod()

Description:

The classmethod() decorator in Python is used to define a class method within a class. A class method is a method that is bound to the class and not to any specific instance of the class. Class methods can be called on the class itself and do not require the creation of an instance. They are often used to perform actions that are related to the class but don't depend on specific instance data.

Syntax:

@classmethod

def method_name(cls, arguments):

  # Method body

- @classmethod: This is a decorator that indicates the following function is a class method.

- method_name: The name of the class method.

- cls: This is a convention for the first parameter of a class method, which refers to the class itself (similar to self for instance methods).

- arguments: The parameters that the class method accepts.

Example of Usage:

```python
class MyClass:
    class_variable = 0

    def __init__(self, value):
        self.instance_variable = value

    @classmethod
    def increment_class_variable(cls):
        cls.class_variable += 1

    def display(self):
        print(f"Instance Variable: {self.instance_variable}")
        print(f"Class Variable: {self.class_variable}")

# Creating instances of MyClass
obj1 = MyClass(10)
obj2 = MyClass(20)

# Accessing the class method to increment the class variable
MyClass.increment_class_variable()
```

Displaying the instance and class variables for obj1

obj1.display()

Displaying the instance and class variables for obj2

obj2.display()

Explanation of the Example:

1. We define a class MyClass with an instance variable instance_variable and a class variable class_variable.

2. The increment_class_variable() method is decorated with @classmethod. It increments the class variable class_variable using the cls parameter.

3. We create two instances of MyClass, obj1 and obj2.

4. We call the increment_class_variable() method on the class MyClass, which increments the class_variable.

5. We display the instance variables and the updated class variable for both obj1 and obj2.

Tips:

- Class methods are bound to the class and not to specific instances. They can be called on the class itself or on any instance of the class.

- The cls parameter in a class method refers to the class itself and is used to access class-level attributes and methods.

- Class methods are often used for tasks that are related to the class as a whole, such as managing class-level data or performing class-level operations.

- Use class methods when you need to modify or access class-level attributes that are shared among all instances of the class.

- Decorate a method with @classmethod to define it as a class method.

- Class methods can be called on the class or on instances of the class, but they cannot directly access instance-specific data (e.g., instance variables) without access via class-level attributes or parameters.

5.3 isinstance()

Description:

The isinstance() function in Python is used to check if an object is an instance of a specified class or a tuple of classes. It is commonly used to determine the type of an object and to perform type checking. isinstance() returns True if the object is an instance of the specified class or one of the specified classes; otherwise, it returns False.

Syntax:

isinstance(object, classinfo)

- object: The object to be checked.

- classinfo: A class or a tuple of classes to check against.

Example of Usage:

 # Example 1: Checking if an object is an instance of a specific class

```
class Dog:
    pass
```

```python
dog = Dog()
result = isinstance(dog, Dog)
print(result)  # Output: True
```

 # Example 2: Checking if an object is an instance of multiple classes

```python
class Cat:
    pass


class Animal:
    pass


cat = Cat()
result = isinstance(cat, (Cat, Animal))
print(result)  # Output: True
```

 # Example 3: Checking if an object is not an instance of a class

```python
class Bird:
    pass


dog = Dog()
result = isinstance(dog, Bird)
print(result)  # Output: False
```

Explanation of the Examples:

1. In Example 1, we define a class Dog and create an instance of it. We use isinstance() to check if the dog object is an instance of the Dog class, which returns True.

2. Example 2 demonstrates checking if an object is an instance of multiple classes. We define two classes, Cat and Animal, and create an instance of Cat. We use isinstance() with a tuple of classes to check if the cat object is an instance of either Cat or Animal, which returns True.

3. Example 3 checks if an object is not an instance of a specified class. We define a class Bird and create an instance of the Dog class. We use isinstance() to check if the dog object is an instance of Bird, which returns False.

Tips:

- isinstance() is a useful tool for performing type checking in your code, especially when you want to ensure that an object is of a certain type before performing operations on it.

- The second argument, classinfo, can be a single class or a tuple of classes. If object is an instance of any of the classes specified in classinfo, isinstance() returns True.

- You can use isinstance() in conditionals to control the flow of your program based on the type of an object.

- Be cautious when using isinstance() with inheritance hierarchies. It returns True not only for the exact class but also for subclasses. If you need to check for an exact class match, consider using the type() function or comparing the class directly.

- Avoid excessive use of isinstance() and prefer using polymorphism and inheritance when designing object-oriented code to improve code maintainability and readability.

5.4 issubclass()

Description:

The issubclass() function in Python is used to check if a class is a subclass of a specified class or a tuple of classes. It is commonly used to determine if one class is derived from another class in the class hierarchy. issubclass() returns True if the class is a subclass of the specified class or one of the specified classes; otherwise, it returns False.

Syntax:

issubclass(class, classinfo)

- class: The class to be checked.

- classinfo: A class or a tuple of classes to check against.

Example of Usage:

 # Example 1: Checking if a class is a subclass of another class

class Animal:

   pass

```python
class Dog(Animal):
    pass


result = issubclass(Dog, Animal)
print(result)  # Output: True
```

Example 2: Checking if a class is a subclass of multiple classes

```python
class Cat:
    pass


class Pet:
    pass


result = issubclass(Cat, (Cat, Pet))
print(result)  # Output: True
```

Example 3: Checking if a class is not a subclass of another class

```python
class Bird:
    pass


result = issubclass(Bird, Dog)
print(result)  # Output: False
```

Explanation of the Examples:

1. In Example 1, we define two classes, Animal and Dog, where Dog is a subclass of Animal. We use issubclass() to check if the Dog class is a subclass of the Animal class, which returns True.

2. Example 2 demonstrates checking if a class is a subclass of multiple classes. We define two classes, Cat and Pet, and use issubclass() with a tuple of classes to check if the Cat class is a subclass of either Cat or Pet, which returns True.

3. Example 3 checks if a class is not a subclass of another class. We define a class Bird, which is not related to the Dog class. We use issubclass() to check if the Bird class is a subclass of Dog, which returns False.

Tips:

- issubclass() is helpful for checking class inheritance relationships in your code, ensuring that a class is a subclass of another class before performing certain operations.

- The second argument, classinfo, can be a single class or a tuple of classes. If the class is a subclass of any of the classes specified in classinfo, issubclass() returns True.

- You can use issubclass() in conditionals to control the flow of your program based on class inheritance relationships.

- Be aware that issubclass() returns True not only for direct subclasses but also for classes further down the inheritance hierarchy. If you need to check for a direct subclass relationship, consider using type() or comparing the class directly.

- It's a good practice to document and design your classes with clear inheritance hierarchies to make use of issubclass() and other tools for managing class relationships effectively.

5.5 property()

Description:

The property() function in Python is used to create a special kind of attribute known as a property. Properties allow you to define custom behavior for accessing and modifying object attributes. By using the property() function as a decorator or calling it as a function, you can specify getter, setter, and deleter methods for an attribute, providing more control and flexibility over how the attribute is accessed and modified.

Syntax:

property(fget=None, fset=None, fdel=None, doc=None)

- fget (optional): A function to get the attribute's value. This function is called when you access the property's value.

- fset (optional): A function to set the attribute's value. This function is called when you assign a new value to the property.

- fdel (optional): A function to delete the attribute. This function is called when you use the del statement to delete the property.

- doc (optional): A docstring that describes the property.

Example of Usage:

```python
class Rectangle:
    def __init__(self, width, height):
        self._width = width
        self._height = height

    @property
    def width(self):
        return self._width

    @width.setter
    def width(self, value):
        if value < 0:
            raise ValueError("Width cannot be negative")
        self._width = value

    @property
    def height(self):
        return self._height

    @height.setter
    def height(self, value):
        if value < 0:
```

```python
        raise ValueError("Height cannot be negative")
    self._height = value


    @property
    def area(self):
        return self._width * self._height


    @property
    def perimeter(self):
        return 2 * (self._width + self._height)


# Creating a Rectangle object
rect = Rectangle(5, 4)


# Accessing properties
print(rect.width)  # Output: 5
print(rect.height)  # Output: 4


# Modifying properties
rect.width = 6
rect.height = 3


# Accessing computed properties
```

print(rect.area) # Output: 18

print(rect.perimeter) # Output: 18

Explanation of the Example:

1. We define a Rectangle class with private attributes _width and _height to store the dimensions of the rectangle.

2. We use the @property decorator to create getter methods (width and height) for accessing the attributes. These methods are called when we access the properties.

3. We use the @width.setter and @height.setter decorators to create setter methods for modifying the attributes. These methods are called when we assign new values to the properties.

4. We also define computed properties (area and perimeter) using the @property decorator. These properties are read-only and calculate values based on the attributes.

5. We create a Rectangle object and demonstrate accessing and modifying the properties.

Tips:

- Use the property() function to create properties with custom getter, setter, and deleter methods.

- Properties are useful for controlling attribute access and implementing computed properties.

- Make sure to use a unique name for the property methods to avoid conflicts with the attribute name.

- Document your properties with clear docstrings to describe their purpose and behavior.

- Properties can be a powerful tool for encapsulating and controlling access to object attributes, providing a more Pythonic way to work with object data.

5.6 staticmethod()

Description:

The staticmethod() function in Python is used to define a static method within a class. Static methods are methods that are bound to the class and not to the instance of the class. They can be called on the class itself without creating an instance of the class. Static methods do not have access to the instance or its attributes, and they do not modify the instance's state.

Syntax:

```
@staticmethod
def method_name(arguments):
    # Method implementation
```

- @staticmethod: This is a decorator that indicates that the following function is a static method.

- method_name: The name of the static method you want to define.

- arguments: The method can take any number of arguments, including none.

Example of Usage:

```python
class MathUtils:

    @staticmethod
    def add(x, y):
        return x + y


    @staticmethod
    def subtract(x, y):
        return x - y


# Calling static methods without creating an instance
sum_result = MathUtils.add(5, 3)
difference_result = MathUtils.subtract(10, 4)


print(sum_result)        # Output: 8
print(difference_result)  # Output: 6
```

Explanation of the Example:

1. We define a MathUtils class with two static methods, add() and subtract(). These methods do not require an instance of the class and can be called directly on the class itself.

2. We call the add() and subtract() static methods using the class name MathUtils without creating an instance of the class. This demonstrates how static methods can be used without needing to instantiate the class.

Tips:

- Use static methods when you have utility functions that are related to a class but do not depend on its instance state.

- Static methods are often used for helper functions and operations that do not require access to instance attributes.

- When defining a static method, you do not need to include self as the first argument. Instead, static methods only accept regular function arguments.

- Static methods are called on the class itself, not on instances of the class. This makes them useful for functions that operate on class-level data or perform general-purpose operations related to the class.

- Be aware that static methods cannot access or modify instance-specific attributes and should not be used when you need access to instance state or behavior.

5.7 super()

Description:

The super() function in Python is used to call a method from a parent or superclass. It is commonly used within the methods of a subclass to invoke methods or constructors of its superclass. This allows you to extend and customize the behavior of inherited methods while still using the functionality provided by the superclass.

Syntax:

super([type[, object-or-type]])

- type (optional): The class type in which to search for a superclass.

- object-or-type (optional): An instance or class type that determines the search start point. If omitted, it defaults to the current instance's class.

Example of Usage:

```python
class Animal:
    def __init__(self, name):
        self.name = name
```

```python
def speak(self):

    pass


class Dog(Animal):

    def __init__(self, name, breed):

        super().__init__(name)  # Call the superclass constructor

        self.breed = breed


    def speak(self):

        return "Woof!"


# Creating a Dog object

dog = Dog("Buddy", "Golden Retriever")


# Accessing attributes

print(dog.name)   # Output: Buddy

print(dog.breed)  # Output: Golden Retriever


# Calling superclass method using super()

superclass_result = super(Dog, dog).speak()

print(superclass_result)  # Output: Woof!
```

Explanation of the Example:

1. We define a Animal class with an __init__() method to initialize the name attribute and a speak() method, which is left empty.

2. We define a Dog class that inherits from Animal. In the Dog class, we override the __init__() method to also initialize the breed attribute and the speak() method to return "Woof!"

3. Inside the Dog class's __init__() method, we use super().__init__(name) to call the constructor of the superclass Animal. This initializes the name attribute inherited from the Animal class.

4. We create a Dog object named dog and demonstrate how to access its attributes, both inherited (name) and specific to the Dog class (breed).

5. We use super(Dog, dog).speak() to call the speak() method of the superclass Animal from within the Dog class. This allows us to access and use the superclass's behavior while still customizing the speak() method for Dog.

Tips:

- super() is commonly used in inheritance to access and call methods or constructors of a superclass from within a subclass.

- When using super(), you typically provide the current class (Dog) and the instance (dog) as arguments to specify where to start the search for the superclass.

- super() is helpful for extending and customizing the behavior of inherited methods while reusing the functionality provided by the superclass.

- Be aware that super() can be used with multiple inheritance to access methods from multiple superclasses. In such cases, the method resolution order (MRO) determines the order in which superclasses are searched.

5.8 type()

Description:

The type() function in Python is used to determine the type or class of an object. It can be used in two ways: to check the type of an object or to create a new class.

1. Checking the Type of an Object:

   - When used with a single argument, type() returns the type or class of that object. It is commonly used to check the type of variables or objects at runtime.

2. Creating a New Class:

   - When used with three arguments, type(name, bases, dict) creates a new class. This form of type() is a metaclass that allows you to dynamically create classes in Python. It takes the following arguments:

     - name: The name of the new class.

     - bases: A tuple of base classes (parent classes).

     - dict: A dictionary containing the class's attributes and methods.

Syntax for Checking Type:

type(object)

Syntax for Creating a New Class:

```python
type(name, bases, dict)
```

Example of Checking Type:

```python
x = 10
y = "Hello"
z = [1, 2, 3]

print(type(x))  # Output: <class 'int'>
print(type(y))  # Output: <class 'str'>
print(type(z))  # Output: <class 'list'>
```

Example of Creating a New Class:

```python
MyClass = type('MyClass', (object,), {'x': 100})
```

Creating an instance of the dynamically created class

obj = MyClass()

print(obj.x) # Output: 100

Explanation of the Example:

1. In the first example, we use type() to check the types of variables x, y, and z.

2. In the second example, we use type() to dynamically create a new class named MyClass. This class has a single attribute x with a value of 100. We then create an instance of MyClass called obj and access its x attribute.

Tips:

- Use type() to check the type of objects, especially when dealing with dynamic or unknown data types.

- For dynamic class creation using type(), provide the class name, base classes (if any), and a dictionary containing attributes and methods.

- Creating classes with type() is powerful but should be used judiciously. In most cases, defining classes using the class keyword is more readable and maintainable.

- The ability to create classes dynamically can be useful in advanced scenarios such as code generation, metaprogramming, and building frameworks.

VI.
Data Manipulation Functions

6.1 delattr()

Description:

The delattr() function in Python is used to delete an attribute from an object. An attribute is a named value associated with an object, and it can be a data attribute or a method attribute (function). This function allows you to remove an attribute, effectively "unbinding" it from the object.

Syntax:

delattr(object, attribute_name)

- object: The object from which you want to delete the attribute.

- attribute_name: The name of the attribute you want to delete.

Example of Usage:

```python
class Person:
    def __init__(self, name, age):
        self.name = name
        self.age = age

# Creating an instance of the Person class
person = Person("Alice", 30)

# Deleting an attribute using delattr()
delattr(person, "age")

# Attempting to access the deleted attribute raises an AttributeError
# print(person.age)  # This line will raise an error

# Deleting a non-existent attribute raises no error
delattr(person, "address")
```

Explanation of the Example:

1. We define a Person class with two data attributes: name and age.

2. We create an instance of the Person class named person with the name "Alice" and age 30.

3. We use delattr(person, "age") to delete the age attribute from the person object.

4. Attempting to access the deleted attribute person.age will raise an AttributeError because the attribute no longer exists.

5. We also demonstrate that using delattr() to delete a non-existent attribute (e.g., "address") does not raise an error.

Tips:

- Be cautious when using delattr() as it permanently removes an attribute from an object.

- Use hasattr(object, attribute_name) to check if an attribute exists before attempting to delete it.

- Deleting attributes from built-in objects (e.g., modifying built-in types like lists or dictionaries) is generally not recommended and can lead to unexpected behavior. It's safer to follow the conventions for modifying built-in objects using their built-in methods.

6.2 getattr()

Description:

The getattr() function in Python is used to retrieve the value of an attribute from an object. An attribute is a named value associated with an object, and it can be a data attribute or a method attribute (function). This function allows you to access the value of an attribute, and it can provide a default value if the attribute does not exist.

Syntax:

getattr(object, attribute_name, default)

- object: The object from which you want to retrieve the attribute.

- attribute_name: The name of the attribute you want to access.

- default (optional): The value to return if the attribute does not exist. If not specified, getattr() raises an AttributeError if the attribute is not found.

Example of Usage:

class Person:

    def __init__(self, name, age):

```python
        self.name = name
        self.age = age


# Creating an instance of the Person class
person = Person("Alice", 30)


# Accessing attributes using getattr()
name = getattr(person, "name")
age = getattr(person, "age")
city = getattr(person, "city", "Unknown")


print("Name:", name)  # Output: Name: Alice
print("Age:", age)    # Output: Age: 30
print("City:", city)  # Output: City: Unknown
```

Explanation of the Example:

1. We define a Person class with two data attributes: name and age.

2. We create an instance of the Person class named person with the name "Alice" and age 30.

3. We use getattr(person, "name") to retrieve the value of the name attribute from the person object, and we store it in the name variable.

4. Similarly, we use getattr(person, "age") to retrieve the value of the age attribute.

5. We also use getattr(person, "city", "Unknown") to retrieve the value of a non-existent attribute, "city," and provide a default value of "Unknown." Since "city" does not exist as an attribute in the person object, the default value "Unknown" is returned.

Tips:

- getattr() is useful when you need to access attributes dynamically or when you want to provide default values for attributes that may or may not exist.

- Be cautious when using getattr() without specifying a default value, as it raises an AttributeError if the attribute does not exist.

- It's a good practice to use hasattr(object, attribute_name) to check if an attribute exists before using getattr() to access it, especially if you are not sure whether the attribute is present in the object.

6.3 setattr()

Description:

The setattr() function in Python is used to set the value of an attribute in an object. An attribute is a named value associated with an object, and it can be a data attribute or a method attribute (function). This function allows you to modify or create attributes within an object.

Syntax:

setattr(object, attribute_name, value)

- object: The object in which you want to set or modify the attribute.

- attribute_name: The name of the attribute you want to set.

- value: The value you want to assign to the attribute.

Example of Usage:

class Person:

   def __init__(self, name, age):

     self.name = name

```python
    self.age = age


# Creating an instance of the Person class
person = Person("Alice", 30)


# Modifying attributes using setattr()
setattr(person, "name", "Bob")
setattr(person, "city", "New York")


print("Name:", person.name)  # Output: Name: Bob
print("Age:", person.age)    # Output: Age: 30
print("City:", getattr(person, "city", "Unknown"))  # Output: City: New York
```

Explanation of the Example:

1. We define a Person class with two data attributes: name and age.

2. We create an instance of the Person class named person with the name "Alice" and age 30.

3. We use setattr(person, "name", "Bob") to modify the value of the name attribute of the person object. As a result, the name attribute now has the value "Bob."

4. We use setattr(person, "city", "New York") to create a new attribute called "city" in the person object and assign it the value "New York."

5. We print the values of the attributes to verify the changes.

Tips:

- setattr() is useful for dynamically modifying or creating attributes within an object.

- Be cautious when using setattr() as it can create new attributes, potentially leading to unexpected behavior.

- It's a good practice to use hasattr(object, attribute_name) to check if an attribute exists before using setattr() to modify it, especially if you are not sure whether the attribute is already present in the object.

- Modifying attributes using setattr() can be a powerful tool for altering object properties dynamically, but it should be used carefully to maintain object integrity and prevent unintended side effects.

6.4 vars()

Description:

The vars() function in Python is used to return the __dict__ attribute of an object. The __dict__ attribute is a dictionary that contains the namespace of an object, including its attributes and their values. This function allows you to access and manipulate the attributes of an object as a dictionary.

Syntax:

vars(object)

- object: The object from which you want to retrieve the __dict__ attribute.

Example of Usage:

```
class Person:
    def __init__(self, name, age):
        self.name = name
        self.age = age
```

```python
# Creating an instance of the Person class

person = Person("Alice", 30)


# Accessing and manipulating attributes using vars()

attributes = vars(person)
print("Attributes:", attributes)


# Modifying an attribute using the vars() dictionary

attributes["name"] = "Bob"


# Accessing the modified attribute

print("Name:", person.name)  # Output: Name: Bob
```

Explanation of the Example:

1. We define a Person class with two data attributes: name and age.

2. We create an instance of the Person class named person with the name "Alice" and age 30.

3. We use vars(person) to access the __dict__ attribute of the person object, which returns a dictionary containing the object's attributes and their values. In this case, the dictionary includes "name": "Alice" and "age": 30.

4. We modify the "name" attribute in the attributes dictionary to "Bob."

5. We print the modified attribute using person.name, and it reflects the change made using the vars() dictionary.

Tips:

- vars() is a convenient way to access and manipulate the attributes of an object as a dictionary.

- Be cautious when using vars() to modify attributes, as it directly alters the object's namespace. It's typically better to use standard attribute access and assignment (object.attribute) whenever possible for clarity and maintainability.

- The __dict__ attribute is not present in all objects. It exists for objects that are instances of classes that have attributes defined with the self.attribute syntax. For objects of classes that don't use this syntax, __dict__ may not be available.

6.5 dir()

Description:

The dir() function in Python is used to retrieve a list of names in the current scope or the attributes of an object. It returns a list of names that are defined in the scope where it is called or, if an object is provided as an argument, it returns a list of attributes and methods of that object.

Syntax:

dir([object])

- object (optional): An object to inspect. If not provided, dir() returns the names in the current scope.

Example of Usage:

1. Using dir() in the current scope:

```
# Define some variables in the current scope
x = 10
```

```python
y = "Hello"

# Get the names in the current scope
names = dir()
print(names)
```

2. Using dir() with an object:

```python
class Person:
    def __init__(self, name, age):
        self.name = name
        self.age = age

# Creating an instance of the Person class
person = Person("Alice", 30)

# Get the attributes and methods of the person object
attributes = dir(person)
print(attributes)
```

Explanation of the Example:

1. In the first example, we define two variables x and y in the current scope. We use dir() without an argument to get the names defined in the current scope. The dir() function returns a list of names, including built-in names and user-defined variables.

2. In the second example, we define a Person class with two attributes (name and age). We create an instance of the Person class named person. We then use dir(person) to get a list of attributes and methods associated with the person object. The list includes both attributes and special methods provided by Python.

Tips:

- dir() is a useful tool for exploring the attributes and methods of an object or inspecting the current scope for defined names.

- When using dir() with an object, it provides a way to discover what attributes and methods are available for that object, which can be especially helpful when working with external libraries or modules.

- Be aware that dir() returns a comprehensive list of names or attributes, including both built-in and user-defined ones. Not all of these may be relevant to your specific use case, so it's important to review the list and focus on the ones you need.

6.6 locals()

Description:

The locals() function in Python is used to retrieve a dictionary representing the current local symbol table. It returns a dictionary of the current local variables, which includes variable names and their corresponding values in the current scope.

Syntax:

```
locals()
```

Example of Usage:

```
def example_function():
    a = 10
    b = "Hello"
    local_vars = locals()
    print(local_vars)

example_function()
```

Explanation of the Example:

In this example, we define a function example_function() that contains two local variables, a and b. Within the function, we call locals() to retrieve a dictionary representing the current local symbol table, which includes the local variables a and b along with their values. We then print the local_vars dictionary.

Output:

{'a': 10, 'b': 'Hello'}

Tips:

- locals() is often used for introspection or debugging purposes when you need to inspect the current state of local variables within a function or code block.

- Keep in mind that locals() returns a dictionary that represents the local symbol table at the time of the function call. If you modify this dictionary, it does not affect the actual local variables. It's typically used for inspection and should not be used to modify local variables.

- While locals() provides information about local variables, it doesn't include global variables, built-in names, or variables from outer scopes. If you need to access global variables or variables from an outer scope, you should use the globals() function or access them directly.

- Be cautious when using locals() in production code, as it is primarily intended for debugging and introspection. Excessive use of locals() can make the code less readable and maintainable.

6.7 globals()

Description:

The globals() function in Python is used to retrieve a dictionary representing the current global symbol table. It returns a dictionary of all global variables, which includes variable names and their corresponding values at the module level.

Syntax:

globals()

Example of Usage:

global_var = "I am a global variable"

def example_function():
    local_var = "I am a local variable"
    global_vars = globals()
    print(global_vars["global_var"])
    print(global_vars.get("local_var"))

example_function()

Explanation of the Example:

In this example, we have a global variable global_var defined at the module level and a local variable local_var defined within the example_function(). Inside the function, we call globals() to retrieve a dictionary representing the current global symbol table, which includes all global variables.

We then attempt to access two variables within the global_vars dictionary:

- We use global_vars["global_var"] to access the global variable global_var, and it prints its value.

- We use global_vars.get("local_var") to access the local variable local_var, but since it is not a global variable, it returns None.

Output:

I am a global variable

None

Tips:

- globals() is useful for introspection or debugging when you need to inspect the state of global variables within a module or script.

- Be aware that globals() returns a dictionary that represents the global symbol table at the time of the function call. If you modify this dictionary, it does not affect the actual global variables. It's typically used for inspection and should not be used to modify global variables.

- Avoid modifying global variables directly using globals(), as it can make the code less maintainable and harder to understand. It's generally recommended to use standard assignment and access methods for global variables.

- While globals() provides information about global variables, it doesn't include local variables from functions or variables from outer scopes. If you need to access local variables within a function or variables from outer scopes, you should use the locals() function or access them directly.

6.8 hash()

Description:

The hash() function in Python is used to generate a hash value for a given object. A hash value is a fixed-size numerical value computed from the content of an object. Hash values are commonly used in data structures like dictionaries and sets to quickly look up and compare objects.

Syntax:

hash(object)

- object: The object for which you want to generate a hash value.

Example of Usage:

Using hash() with integers

hash_value_1 = hash(42)

hash_value_2 = hash(1000)

```
# Using hash() with strings

hash_value_3 = hash("hello")

hash_value_4 = hash("world")


# Using hash() with tuples

hash_value_5 = hash((1, 2, 3))


print(hash_value_1)

print(hash_value_2)

print(hash_value_3)

print(hash_value_4)

print(hash_value_5)
```

Explanation of the Example:

In this example, we use the hash() function to generate hash values for different types of objects:

- hash(42) and hash(1000) generate hash values for integers.

- hash("hello") and hash("world") generate hash values for strings.

- hash((1, 2, 3)) generates a hash value for a tuple.

Each time we call hash() with an object, it computes a hash value based on the content of the object. Note that hash values may vary depending on the Python implementation and may change between Python sessions.

Tips:

- The hash() function is commonly used when working with dictionaries and sets to efficiently store and look up values based on their hash values. It helps improve the performance of data retrieval.

- Not all objects in Python are hashable. Only immutable objects (e.g., numbers, strings, tuples) are hashable. Mutable objects (e.g., lists, dictionaries) are not hashable because their content can change, leading to inconsistent hash values.

- Hash values are not guaranteed to be unique for different objects. Collisions can occur, where different objects produce the same hash value. However, Python's hash functions are designed to minimize collisions for common types.

- When using custom objects as keys in dictionaries or elements in sets, it's important to define the __hash__() method for those objects to ensure proper hashability and consistent behavior.

6.9 help()

Description:

The help() function in Python is used to access built-in documentation and information about objects, modules, functions, classes, methods, and keywords. It provides helpful information and documentation strings (docstrings) associated with Python objects.

Syntax:

help([object])

- object (optional): The object or module you want to get help on. If not provided, it starts an interactive help session.

Example of Usage:

1. Using help() without an argument to start an interactive help session:

help()

2. Using help() with an object, function, or module to get information:

```python
# Get help on a built-in function
help(len)


# Get help on a module
import math
help(math)


# Get help on a class
help(list)


# Get help on a specific object or instance
my_list = [1, 2, 3]
help(my_list)


# Get help on a keyword (e.g., "if")
help("if")
```

Explanation of the Example:

- In the first example, calling help() without an argument starts an interactive help session where you can type the name of the object or topic you want help with.

- In the other examples, we use help() with various arguments to retrieve information about different Python objects:

  - help(len) provides information about the built-in len() function.

  - help(math) provides information about the math module.

  - help(list) provides information about the list class.

  - help(my_list) provides information about the my_list object, which is an instance of the list class.

  - help("if") provides information about the Python if keyword.

Tips:

- The help() function is a valuable tool for exploring Python's built-in functionality and getting detailed documentation on how to use various objects and modules.

- When you enter the interactive help session by calling help() without an argument, you can exit by typing quit or pressing Ctrl+D (Unix/Linux) or Ctrl+Z (Windows).

- You can use help() to explore third-party libraries and modules by importing them and then calling help() on them.

- Many Python objects, modules, functions, and classes have docstrings that provide detailed explanations and examples of usage. Using help() to access these docstrings can be very helpful when learning and working with Python.

6.10 id()

Description:

The id() function in Python is used to get the unique identifier (identity) of an object. This identifier is an integer that represents the memory address of the object. Each object in Python has a unique identity, and this identity remains constant throughout the object's lifetime.

Syntax:

id(object)

- object: The object for which you want to obtain the unique identifier.

Example of Usage:

```python
# Using id() with integers
x = 42
y = 42
id_x = id(x)
id_y = id(y)
```

```python
# Using id() with strings
name1 = "Alice"
name2 = "Alice"
id_name1 = id(name1)
id_name2 = id(name2)


# Using id() with lists
list1 = [1, 2, 3]
list2 = [1, 2, 3]
id_list1 = id(list1)
id_list2 = id(list2)


print(id_x)
print(id_y)
print(id_name1)
print(id_name2)
print(id_list1)
print(id_list2)
```

Explanation of the Example:

In this example, we use the id() function to obtain the unique identifiers of various objects:

- For integers, x and y have the same value, but they may or may not have the same identity, depending on Python's optimization. In this case, they have the same identity because Python caches small integers for efficiency.

- For strings, name1 and name2 have the same value and the same identity because Python caches string literals with the same content.

- For lists, list1 and list2 have the same value, but they have different identities because lists are mutable, and each instance is a separate object.

Tips:

- The id() function is primarily used for debugging and understanding how Python manages objects in memory. It's useful for checking whether two variables reference the same object or not.

- While two objects with the same value may have the same identity in some cases (e.g., small integers or cached string literals), it's not a general rule. In most cases, objects with the same value will have different identities.

- Python's memory management system takes care of creating and deallocating memory for objects. You don't need to worry about memory management details in most Python programs. Use id() for debugging and understanding, not for typical application logic.

6.11 type()

Description:

The type() function in Python is used to get the type or class of an object. It returns the type of the object as a class object, which can be used to determine the data type or class of the given object. This function is often used for introspection and checking the data type of variables.

Syntax:

type(object)

- object: The object for which you want to determine the data type or class.

Example of Usage:

```
# Using type() with various objects
x = 42
y = "Hello, World!"
z = [1, 2, 3]
w = {"name": "Alice", "age": 30}
```

```python
# Determine the data type of each object

type_x = type(x)

type_y = type(y)

type_z = type(z)

type_w = type(w)


print(type_x)  # <class 'int'>

print(type_y)  # <class 'str'>

print(type_z)  # <class 'list'>

print(type_w)  # <class 'dict'>
```

Explanation of the Example:

In this example, we use the type() function to determine the data type or class of various objects:

- type_x will be <class 'int'> because x is an integer.

- type_y will be <class 'str'> because y is a string.

- type_z will be <class 'list'> because z is a list.

- type_w will be <class 'dict'> because w is a dictionary.

Tips:

- The type() function is useful for checking the data type of an object, especially when you want to perform different operations based on the type of the object.

- You can use the isinstance() function to check if an object is an instance of a particular class or type.

- While type() is useful for introspection and debugging, it's important not to rely excessively on type checking in Python. Python's dynamic typing and duck typing encourage writing code that works with objects based on their behavior rather than their specific types.

6.12 input()

Description:

The input() function in Python is used to take user input from the keyboard. It allows a program to pause and wait for the user to enter some text or data, which is then returned as a string. This function is commonly used when you need to interact with the user and collect information or commands from them.

Syntax:

input(prompt)

- prompt (optional): A string that is displayed to the user as a prompt before waiting for input. It provides guidance or instructions to the user about what input is expected.

Example of Usage:

```
# Using input() to get user input
name = input("Enter your name: ")
age = input("Enter your age: ")
```

```
# Displaying the user's input
print("Hello, " + name + "!")
print("You are " + age + " years old.")
```

Explanation of the Example:

In this example, the input() function is used to collect user input:

- The first call to input("Enter your name: ") displays the prompt "Enter your name: " to the user, and the user is expected to enter their name. The input is stored in the variable name.

- The second call to input("Enter your age: ") displays the prompt "Enter your age: " to the user, and the user is expected to enter their age. The input is stored in the variable age.

The user's input is then displayed back to the user with a greeting.

Tips:

- The input() function always returns a string, even if the user enters a numeric value. If you need to use the input as a numeric value (e.g., an integer or a float), you should convert it using int() or float().

- Be cautious when using input() in production code, especially if the input is used in critical parts of your program. You should validate and sanitize user input to prevent potential security vulnerabilities or errors.

- You can use the strip() method to remove leading and trailing whitespace characters from the input, which can be helpful to clean up user input. For example, name = input("Enter your name: ").strip() will remove extra spaces before and after the entered name.

- In Python 2.x, the equivalent function is raw_input(). In Python 3.x, input() replaces raw_input() and behaves as described here.

6.13 open()

Description:

The open() function in Python is used to open files for reading, writing, or both. It allows you to work with files in various modes and provides a way to interact with the contents of a file. The open() function returns a file object that can be used to perform file-related operations.

Syntax:

open(file, mode='r', buffering=-1, encoding=None, errors=None, newline=None, closefd=True, opener=None)

- file: The name of the file to be opened, including its path (if necessary).

- mode (optional): The mode in which the file should be opened. It can be one of the following:

  - 'r': Read (default mode). Opens the file for reading.

  - 'w': Write. Opens the file for writing, creating a new file if it doesn't exist or truncating the existing file.

  - 'a': Append. Opens the file for writing, but appends data to the end of the file if it exists.

  - 'x': Exclusive creation. Opens the file for writing but fails if the file already exists.

  - 'b': Binary mode. Reads or writes the file in binary mode (e.g., 'rb' or 'wb').

  - 't': Text mode (default mode). Reads or writes the file as a text file (e.g., 'rt' or 'wt').

- Other optional parameters like buffering, encoding, errors, newline, closefd, and opener can also be specified for more advanced file operations.

Example of Usage:

```python
# Opening a file for reading and reading its contents
file_name = "sample.txt"
try:
    file = open(file_name, 'r')
    content = file.read()
    print(content)
finally:
    file.close()


# Opening a file for writing and writing data to it
output_file_name = "output.txt"
try:
    output_file = open(output_file_name, 'w')
    output_file.write("Hello, World!\n")
    output_file.write("This is a test file.")
finally:
    output_file.close()
```

Explanation of the Example:

In this example:

1. We use open() to open a file named "sample.txt" in read mode ('r') and read its contents using file.read(). We then print the content to the console.

2. We use open() to open a file named "output.txt" in write mode ('w') and write some text to it using output_file.write(). We close the file after writing.

Tips:

- It's recommended to use the with statement (context manager) when working with files to ensure that the file is properly closed when you're done. This eliminates the need for explicit file.close() calls.

- Be careful when opening files in write mode ('w') as it will overwrite the content of an existing file without warning. Use it with caution.

- You can specify the full path of the file to be opened if it's not in the same directory as your Python script.

- When reading or writing text files, it's a good practice to specify the encoding (e.g., 'utf-8') to ensure compatibility with different character encodings.

- To iterate through the lines of a text file, you can use a for loop with the file object. For example, for line in file: will iterate through each line in the file.

- For reading large files, consider reading them line by line or using the readline() method to avoid loading the entire file into memory at once.

6.14 print()

Description:

The print() function in Python is used to display text or other data to the standard output (usually the console or terminal). It allows you to output information, variables, and messages to the screen for debugging, user interaction, or informative purposes.

Syntax:

print(*objects, sep=' ', end='\n', file=sys.stdout, flush=False)

- *objects (optional): Zero or more objects to be printed. You can specify multiple objects separated by commas.

- sep (optional): The separator to be used between the objects when they are printed. By default, it's a space ' '.

- end (optional): The string to be appended at the end of the printed output. By default, it's a newline character '\n', which means each print call ends with a newline.

- file (optional): The file-like object where the output will be sent. By default, it's sys.stdout, which represents the standard output (usually the console).

- flush (optional): A boolean value that controls whether the output should be flushed immediately. Flushing means forcing the data to be written to the output immediately. By default, it's False.

Example of Usage:

```python
# Printing a simple message
print("Hello, World!")

# Printing variables and formatting output
name = "Alice"
age = 30
print("Name:", name)
print("Age:", age)

# Specifying custom separators and ending characters
print("One", "Two", "Three", sep=', ', end='!\n')

# Redirecting output to a file
with open("output.txt", "w") as file:
    print("This will be written to the file.", file=file)

# Flushing output immediately
print("Flushing...", end='', flush=True)
```

Explanation of the Example:

In this example:

1. We use print() to display a simple message, variables (name and age), and custom separators and ending characters.

2. We redirect the output of print() to a file named "output.txt" using the file parameter.

3. We demonstrate the flush parameter by printing "Flushing..." without a newline and flushing the output immediately.

Tips:

- The print() function is a versatile tool for displaying information during development, debugging, and creating user-friendly command-line interfaces.

- You can use string formatting techniques (e.g., f-strings or the str.format() method) to format the output when printing variables and values.

- To write formatted data to a file, use print() with the file parameter, as shown in the example.

- When working with the sep and end parameters, you can customize how the output is formatted to suit your needs.

- To avoid printing a newline character at the end of a print statement, set end=''.

- Be cautious when using the flush parameter with True, as it can affect performance. Only use it when necessary.

6.15 slice()

Description:

The slice() function in Python is used to create a slice object, which is used to specify how to slice a sequence (such as a list, tuple, or string) using the extended slicing syntax. Slicing allows you to extract a portion of a sequence based on a start, stop, and step.

Syntax:

slice(stop)

slice(start, stop)

slice(start, stop, step)

- start (optional): The starting index of the slice (inclusive). If not provided, it defaults to 0.

- stop: The ending index of the slice (exclusive).

- step (optional): The step or stride used for slicing. If not provided, it defaults to 1.

The slice() function returns a slice object that you can use with sequences like lists, tuples, and strings to extract specific elements.

Example of Usage:

```python
# Creating a slice object

my_slice = slice(2, 5)


# Using the slice object to slice a list

my_list = [1, 2, 3, 4, 5, 6, 7, 8]

result = my_list[my_slice]

print(result)  # Output: [3, 4, 5]


# Slicing a string using a slice object

my_string = "Python Programming"

substring = my_string[slice(7, 18)]

print(substring)  # Output: Programming


# Creating a slice object with step

my_slice = slice(1, 10, 2)

my_list = [0, 1, 2, 3, 4, 5, 6, 7, 8, 9]

result = my_list[my_slice]

print(result)  # Output: [1, 3, 5, 7, 9]
```

Explanation of the Example:

In this example:

1. We create a slice object, my_slice, using the slice() function with different parameters.

2. We use the my_slice object to slice a list, my_list, to extract a portion of the list based on the slice criteria.

3. We also use the slice object directly to slice a string, my_string, to extract a substring.

4. Finally, we create a slice object with a step and use it to slice a list, extracting elements with a specific step.

Tips:

- Slice objects are useful when you need to repeatedly apply the same slice to multiple sequences.

- Slicing in Python is a powerful feature for working with sequences, allowing you to extract portions of data efficiently.

- Remember that the start index is inclusive, while the stop index is exclusive when slicing.

- The step value controls the spacing between elements in the slice.

VII.
String Formatting Functions

7.1 format()

Description:

The format() function in Python is used for string formatting. It allows you to create formatted strings by replacing placeholders with values or expressions. String formatting is a way to control the appearance of the output strings, making them more readable and informative.

Syntax:

```
formatted_string = "some text with {} and {}".format(value1, value2)
```

- "some text with {} and {}": This is a string containing placeholders enclosed in curly braces {}.

- value1 and value2: These are the values or expressions that will replace the placeholders in the order they appear.

The format() function can also use named placeholders and other formatting options to control the appearance of the output string.

Example of Usage:

```python
name = "Alice"
age = 30

# Using positional placeholders
formatted_str = "Hello, my name is {} and I am {} years old.".format(name, age)
print(formatted_str)
# Output: Hello, my name is Alice and I am 30 years old.

# Using named placeholders
formatted_str = "Hello, my name is {name} and I am {age} years old.".format(name=name, age=age)
print(formatted_str)
# Output: Hello, my name is Alice and I am 30 years old.

# Formatting floating-point numbers
pi = 3.14159265359
formatted_float = "The value of pi is approximately {:.2f}".format(pi)
print(formatted_float)
# Output: The value of pi is approximately 3.14
```

Explanation of the Example:

In this example:

1. We create a string with placeholders using {} and then use the format() function to replace the placeholders with values.

2. We can use either positional or named placeholders to specify which values should replace which placeholders.

3. In the last example, we format a floating-point number pi to display it with two decimal places using the :.2f format specifier.

Tips:

- The format() function provides a powerful and flexible way to format strings in Python.

- You can use various formatting options within the placeholders to control the appearance of the output.

- The order of placeholders in the string must match the order of values passed to format(), unless you use named placeholders.

- Python also provides f-strings (formatted string literals) starting from Python 3.6, which offer a more concise way of string formatting.

Description:

The count() method in Python is used for counting the occurrences of a substring within a given string. It searches for the specified substring in the target string and returns the number of times the substring appears. This method is useful when you need to find out how many times a particular substring occurs in a larger text.

Syntax:

count = string.count(substring, start, end)

- string: This is the target string in which you want to search for the substring.

- substring: This is the substring you want to count within the target string.

- start (optional): This is the starting index for the search within the target string. By default, it starts from the beginning of the string.

- end (optional): This is the ending index for the search within the target string. By default, it searches until the end of the string.

Example of Usage:

text = "Python is a powerful programming language. Python is also easy to learn."

Count the occurrences of "Python" in the text

count = text.count("Python")

print("Occurrences of 'Python':", count)

Output: Occurrences of 'Python': 2

Count the occurrences of "Python" in the first part of the text

count = text.count("Python", 0, 28)

print("Occurrences of 'Python' in the first part:", count)

Output: Occurrences of 'Python' in the first part: 1

Explanation of the Example:

In this example:

1. We have a text string text that contains two occurrences of the word "Python."

2. We use the count() method to count the occurrences of "Python" in the entire string and also in the first part of the string by specifying the start and end indices.

Tips:

- The count() method is case-sensitive, so it distinguishes between uppercase and lowercase characters. If you want a case-insensitive search, you can convert the string and substring to lowercase (or uppercase) before using count().

- If the substring is not found in the string, count() returns 0.

- Be cautious with the start and end arguments to ensure that you are searching within the intended portion of the string.

- This method is particularly useful when you need to analyze or manipulate text data by counting specific patterns or words.

7.3 endswith()

Description:

The endswith() method in Python is used to check whether a given string ends with a specified suffix. It returns True if the string ends with the specified suffix and False otherwise. This method is often used to perform conditional checks on string endings.

Syntax:

result = string.endswith(suffix, start, end)

- string: This is the target string that you want to check.

- suffix: This is the substring or suffix you want to check if the target string ends with.

- start (optional): This is the starting index for the search within the target string. By default, it starts from the beginning of the string.

- end (optional): This is the ending index for the search within the target string. By default, it searches until the end of the string.

Example of Usage:

file_name = "document.txt"

Check if the file name ends with ".txt"

result = file_name.endswith(".txt")

print("Ends with .txt:", result)

Output: Ends with .txt: True

Check if the file name ends with ".pdf"

result = file_name.endswith(".pdf")

print("Ends with .pdf:", result)

Output: Ends with .pdf: False

Check if a portion of the file name ends with ".txt"

result = file_name.endswith(".txt", 0, 8)

print("Ends with .txt (partial check):", result)

Output: Ends with .txt (partial check): True

Explanation of the Example:

In this example:

1. We have a file_name string containing the name of a file.

2. We use the endswith() method to check if the file name ends with specific suffixes (".txt" and ".pdf").

3. We also perform a partial check using the start and end arguments to check only a portion of the string.

Tips:

- The endswith() method is case-sensitive, so it distinguishes between uppercase and lowercase characters. If you want a case-insensitive check, you can convert both the string and the suffix to lowercase (or uppercase) before using endswith().

- It's important to specify the correct suffix when using this method to ensure accurate checks.

- This method is commonly used when working with file extensions or when validating file names in a program.

7.4 startswith()

Description:

The startswith() method in Python is used to check whether a given string starts with a specified prefix. It returns True if the string starts with the specified prefix and False otherwise. This method is often used to perform conditional checks on string beginnings.

Syntax:

result = string.startswith(prefix, start, end)

- string: This is the target string that you want to check.

- prefix: This is the substring or prefix you want to check if the target string starts with.

- start (optional): This is the starting index for the search within the target string. By default, it starts from the beginning of the string.

- end (optional): This is the ending index for the search within the target string. By default, it searches until the end of the string.

Example of Usage:

text = "Hello, world!"

```python
# Check if the text starts with "Hello"
result = text.startswith("Hello")
print("Starts with Hello:", result)
# Output: Starts with Hello: True


# Check if the text starts with "hello" (case-sensitive)
result = text.startswith("hello")
print("Starts with hello:", result)
# Output: Starts with hello: False


# Check if a portion of the text starts with "world"
result = text.startswith("world", 7)
print("Starts with world (partial check):", result)
# Output: Starts with world (partial check): True
```

Explanation of the Example:

In this example:

1. We have a text string containing a message.

2. We use the startswith() method to check if the text starts with specific prefixes ("Hello" and "hello").

3. We also perform a partial check using the start argument to check only a portion of the string.

Tips:

- The startswith() method is case-sensitive, so it distinguishes between uppercase and lowercase characters. If you want a case-insensitive check, you can convert both the string and the prefix to lowercase (or uppercase) before using startswith().

- It's important to specify the correct prefix when using this method to ensure accurate checks.

- This method is commonly used when parsing text or validating input in a program.

7.5 find()

Description:

The find() method in Python is used to find the first occurrence of a substring (or a character) in a given string. It returns the lowest index (position) where the substring is found within the string. If the substring is not found, it returns -1. This method is often used to search for specific content within a string.

Syntax:

position = string.find(substring, start, end)

- string: This is the target string in which you want to search for the substring.

- substring: This is the substring you want to find within the target string.

- start (optional): This is the starting index for the search within the target string. By default, it starts from the beginning of the string.

- end (optional): This is the ending index for the search within the target string. By default, it searches until the end of the string.

Example of Usage:

text = "Python is a powerful programming language."

```python
# Find the position of "is" in the text
position = text.find("is")
print("Position of 'is':", position)
# Output: Position of 'is': 7

# Find the position of "programming" (case-sensitive)
position = text.find("programming")
print("Position of 'programming':", position)
# Output: Position of 'programming': 23

# Find the position of "language" with a custom start index
position = text.find("language", 20)
print("Position of 'language' (custom start index):", position)
# Output: Position of 'language' (custom start index): 29

# Find the position of "Java" (substring not found)
position = text.find("Java")
print("Position of 'Java':", position)
# Output: Position of 'Java': -1
```

Explanation of the Example:

In this example:

1. We have a text string containing a sentence.

2. We use the find() method to locate the positions of different substrings ("is," "programming," "language," and "Java").

3. When the substring is found, the method returns the index of its first occurrence. If the substring is not found, it returns -1.

Tips:

- The find() method is case-sensitive, meaning it distinguishes between uppercase and lowercase characters. If you want a case-insensitive search, you can convert both the string and the substring to lowercase (or uppercase) before using find().

- If you want to find all occurrences of a substring, you can use a loop in combination with find() to iteratively search for the substring.

- You can also use the index() method to find the position of a substring, but it raises a ValueError if the substring is not found, while find() returns -1.

7.6 index()

Description:

The index() method in Python is used to find the first occurrence of a substring (or a character) in a given string, similar to the find() method. However, there is a key difference: if the substring is not found, the index() method raises a ValueError, while the find() method returns -1.

Syntax:

position = string.index(substring, start, end)

- string: This is the target string in which you want to search for the substring.

- substring: This is the substring you want to find within the target string.

- start (optional): This is the starting index for the search within the target string. By default, it starts from the beginning of the string.

- end (optional): This is the ending index for the search within the target string. By default, it searches until the end of the string.

Example of Usage:

text = "Python is a powerful programming language."

# Find the position of "is" in the text
position = text.index("is")
print("Position of 'is':", position)
# Output: Position of 'is': 7

# Find the position of "programming" (case-sensitive)
position = text.index("programming")
print("Position of 'programming':", position)
# Output: Position of 'programming': 23

# Find the position of "language" with a custom start index
position = text.index("language", 20)
print("Position of 'language' (custom start index):", position)
# Output: Position of 'language' (custom start index): 29

# Attempt to find the position of "Java" (substring not found)
try:
    position = text.index("Java")
    print("Position of 'Java':", position)
except ValueError as e:
    print("Substring not found:", e)
# Output: Substring not found: substring not found

Explanation of the Example:

In this example:

1. We have a text string containing a sentence.

2. We use the index() method to locate the positions of different substrings ("is," "programming," "language," and "Java").

3. When the substring is found, the method returns the index of its first occurrence. If the substring is not found, it raises a ValueError.

Tips:

- Use the index() method when you want to ensure that the substring is found in the string. If the substring may or may not be present, consider using the find() method, which returns -1 if the substring is not found.

- To handle the case where the substring is not found with the index() method, wrap the call in a try...except block to catch the ValueError.

Description:

The join() method in Python is used to concatenate elements of an iterable (e.g., a list, tuple, or string) into a single string, with a specified separator between each element. It is a powerful way to create strings from a sequence of items.

Syntax:

result_string = separator.join(iterable)

- separator: This is the string that will be used to separate the elements in the iterable when they are concatenated into the result string.

- iterable: This is the iterable (e.g., list, tuple, or string) whose elements you want to join into a single string.

Example of Usage:

 # Example 1: Joining elements of a list into a string

fruits = ["apple", "banana", "cherry"]

result = ", ".join(fruits)

print(result)

Output: apple, banana, cherry

 # Example 2: Joining characters of a string with a custom separator

text = "Python is awesome"

result = "_".join(text)

print(result)

Output: P_y_t_h_o_n_ _i_s_ _a_w_e_s_o_m_e

 # Example 3: Joining numbers as strings with a custom separator

numbers = ["1", "2", "3", "4", "5"]

result = " | ".join(numbers)

print(result)

Output: 1 | 2 | 3 | 4 | 5

Explanation of the Examples:

1. In Example 1, we have a list of fruits, and we use the join() method with ", " as the separator to concatenate the elements of the list into a single string.

2. In Example 2, we have a text string, and we use the join() method with "_" as the separator to concatenate the characters of the string into a single string.

3. In Example 3, we have a list of numbers represented as strings, and we use the join() method with " | " as the separator to concatenate the elements of the list into a single string.

Tips:

- The join() method is a powerful way to concatenate elements of an iterable into a string, with full control over the separator.

- Make sure that all elements in the iterable are of type string, as the join() method works with strings. If there are non-string elements, you can convert them to strings using list comprehensions or other methods.

- Be mindful of the separator you choose to use. It should be a string that separates the joined elements in a meaningful way for your application.

- The join() method is more efficient than using a loop to concatenate strings, especially when dealing with a large number of elements, as it avoids the overhead of multiple string copies.

7.8 lower()

Description:

The lower() method in Python is used to convert all characters in a string to lowercase. This is particularly useful when you want to perform case-insensitive string operations, as it standardizes the case of all characters in the string.

Syntax:

lowercase_string = original_string.lower()

- original_string: This is the string that you want to convert to lowercase.

Example of Usage:

 # Example 1: Converting a string to lowercase

text = "Hello, World!"

lower_text = text.lower()

print(lower_text)

Output: hello, world!

Example 2: Case-insensitive string comparison

```python
input_str = "Python"

compare_str = "python"

if input_str.lower() == compare_str.lower():

    print("Strings are equal (case-insensitive)")

else:

    print("Strings are not equal (case-insensitive)")

# Output: Strings are equal (case-insensitive)
```

Explanation of the Examples:

1. In Example 1, we have a string text containing both uppercase and lowercase characters. We use the lower() method to convert the entire string to lowercase.

2. In Example 2, we want to compare two strings, input_str and compare_str, in a case-insensitive manner. To do this, we convert both strings to lowercase using lower() and then perform the comparison. As a result, the strings are considered equal in a case-insensitive comparison.

Tips:

- The lower() method is useful for making string operations case-insensitive, such as string comparisons and searches.

- Keep in mind that lower() does not modify the original string but returns a new string with all characters in lowercase.

- Be cautious when using lower() for case-insensitive comparisons, as it may not handle all language-specific cases perfectly. Some languages have unique casing rules, and you might need to use specialized libraries or techniques for accurate case-insensitive comparisons.

7.9 lstrip()

Description:

The lstrip() method in Python is used to remove leading (leftmost) whitespace characters from the beginning of a string. Whitespace characters include spaces, tabs, and newline characters.

Syntax:

new_string = original_string.lstrip([characters])

- original_string: This is the string from which you want to remove leading whitespace characters.

- characters (optional): This is an optional argument that specifies a set of characters to remove from the left side of the string. If not provided, it defaults to removing all whitespace characters.

Example of Usage:

 # Example 1: Removing leading spaces

text = "   Hello, World!"

new_text = text.lstrip()

print(new_text)

Output: "Hello, World!"

 # Example 2: Removing a specific character from the left

text = "///Python///"

new_text = text.lstrip("/")

print(new_text)

Output: "Python///"

Explanation of the Examples:

1. In Example 1, the lstrip() method is used to remove leading spaces from the string text. The resulting string new_text does not have any leading spaces.

2. In Example 2, the lstrip() method is used with a specific character ("/") as an argument. It removes all leading occurrences of the specified character from the left side of the string.

Tips:

- The lstrip() method is particularly useful when dealing with input data where leading whitespace characters should be ignored or removed.

- If you do not provide the characters argument, lstrip() will remove all leading whitespace characters by default.

- The lstrip() method does not modify the original string but returns a new string with leading characters removed.

- There is a related method called rstrip(), which removes trailing (rightmost) whitespace characters from the end of a string.

7.10 replace()

Description:

The replace() method in Python is used to create a new string by replacing all occurrences of a specified substring (or character) with another substring in a given string. It does not modify the original string but returns a new string with the replacements made.

Syntax:

new_string = original_string.replace(old_substring, new_substring, count)

- original_string: This is the string in which you want to perform replacements.

- old_substring: This is the substring you want to find and replace.

- new_substring: This is the substring that will replace the occurrences of old_substring.

- count (optional): This is an optional parameter that specifies the maximum number of replacements to make. If not provided, all occurrences are replaced.

Example of Usage:

 # Example 1: Simple string replacement

text = "I like ice cream, and I like chocolate ice cream."

new_text = text.replace("ice cream", "gelato")

print(new_text)

Output: "I like gelato, and I like chocolate gelato."

Example 2: Replacing a specified number of occurrences

text = "one, two, three, four, five, five, six"

new_text = text.replace("five", "5", 1)

print(new_text)

Output: "one, two, three, four, 5, five, six"

Explanation of the Examples:

1. In Example 1, the replace() method is used to replace all occurrences of "ice cream" with "gelato" in the string text. The resulting string new_text contains the replacements.

2. In Example 2, the replace() method is used with the count argument set to 1. This means that only the first occurrence of "five" is replaced with "5". The remaining occurrences are not replaced.

Tips:

- The replace() method is a powerful tool for modifying strings, such as cleaning and formatting data.

- If you want to replace all occurrences, you can omit the count parameter or set it to a large number.

- The replace() method creates a new string with the replacements; it does not modify the original string.

- If the old_substring is not found in the original_string, the method returns the original string without changes.

- The replace() method is case-sensitive; it distinguishes between uppercase and lowercase characters.

7.11 rfind()

Description:

The rfind() method in Python is used to find the highest (rightmost) index of a specified substring in a given string. It searches the string from right to left and returns the index of the first occurrence of the substring within the specified range. If the substring is not found, it returns -1.

Syntax:

index = string.rfind(substring, start, end)

- string: This is the string in which you want to search for the substring.

- substring: This is the substring you want to find.

- start (optional): This is the starting index from where the search begins. The default value is 0.

- end (optional): This is the ending index where the search stops. The default value is the length of the string.

Example of Usage:

 # Example 1: Finding the highest index of a substring

text = "Hello, world. Welcome to the world of Python."

index = text.rfind("world")

print(index)

Output: 33

Example 2: Specifying a custom search range

text = "This is an example of an example."

index = text.rfind("example", 0, 15)

print(index)

Output: -1 (substring not found in the specified range)

Explanation of the Examples:

1. In Example 1, the rfind() method is used to find the highest index of the substring "world" in the string text. Since "world" occurs twice in the string, it returns the index of the last occurrence, which is 33.

2. In Example 2, the rfind() method is used with a custom search range specified by the start and end parameters. It searches for "example" within the first 15 characters of the string. Since "example" is not found in this range, it returns -1.

Tips:

- The rfind() method is similar to the find() method but searches from right to left.

- If the substring is not found, the method returns -1.

- You can specify custom search ranges by using the start and end parameters.

- When searching for substrings, keep in mind that Python is case-sensitive, so "example" and "Example" are considered different substrings.

- The rfind() method is useful when you need to find the last occurrence of a substring in a string.

7.12 rindex()

Description:

The rindex() method in Python is used to find the highest (rightmost) index of a specified substring in a given string. It works similarly to the rfind() method but raises a ValueError if the substring is not found instead of returning -1.

Syntax:

index = string.rindex(substring, start, end)

- string: This is the string in which you want to search for the substring.

- substring: This is the substring you want to find.

- start (optional): This is the starting index from where the search begins. The default value is 0.

- end (optional): This is the ending index where the search stops. The default value is the length of the string.

Example of Usage:

 # Example 1: Finding the highest index of a substring

text = "Hello, world. Welcome to the world of Python."

index = text.rindex("world")

print(index)

Output: 33

Example 2: Specifying a custom search range

text = "This is an example of an example."

index = text.rindex("example", 0, 15)

print(index)

Output: ValueError (substring not found in the specified range)

Explanation of the Examples:

1. In Example 1, the rindex() method is used to find the highest index of the substring "world" in the string text. Since "world" occurs twice in the string, it returns the index of the last occurrence, which is 33.

2. In Example 2, the rindex() method is used with a custom search range specified by the start and end parameters. It searches for "example" within the first 15 characters of the string. Since "example" is not found in this range, it raises a ValueError.

Tips:

- The rindex() method is similar to the rfind() method but raises a ValueError if the substring is not found.

- Use try and except blocks to handle the ValueError raised by rindex() if you expect that the substring may not always be present in the string.

- When searching for substrings, keep in mind that Python is case-sensitive, so "example" and "Example" are considered different substrings.

7.13 rstrip()

Description:

The rstrip() method in Python is used to remove trailing (rightmost) whitespace characters from the end of a string. Whitespace characters include spaces, tabs, and newline characters. It returns a new string with trailing whitespace removed.

Syntax:

new_string = string.rstrip([characters])

- string: This is the string from which you want to remove trailing whitespace.

- characters (optional): This is an optional parameter that allows you to specify a set of characters to remove from the end of the string. If provided, it will remove characters from the end until a character not in the specified set is encountered.

Example of Usage:

 # Example 1: Removing trailing whitespace

text = "   Hello, world.   \n"

new_text = text.rstrip()

print(new_text)

Output: "   Hello, world."

Example 2: Removing specific characters from the end

text = "Hello, world!!!"

new_text = text.rstrip("!")

print(new_text)

Output: "Hello, world"

Example 3: Removing both spaces and exclamation marks

text = " Hello, world!!! "

new_text = text.rstrip(" !")

print(new_text)

Output: " Hello, world"

Explanation of the Examples:

1. In Example 1, the rstrip() method is used to remove trailing spaces and newline characters from the end of the string text. The resulting string has no trailing whitespace.

2. In Example 2, the rstrip() method is used with a specific set of characters, "!", provided as an argument. It removes all trailing exclamation marks from the end of the string.

3. In Example 3, the rstrip() method is used with a set of characters containing both spaces and exclamation marks. It removes any trailing spaces or exclamation marks from the end of the string.

Tips:

- The rstrip() method is useful for cleaning up strings by removing unnecessary whitespace at the end.

- It does not modify the original string but returns a new string with the trailing whitespace removed.

- If no characters are provided as an argument, rstrip() will remove all whitespace characters.

- To remove leading (leftmost) whitespace characters, you can use the lstrip() method.

- To remove both leading and trailing whitespace characters, you can use the strip() method.

7.14 split()

Description:

The split() method in Python is used to split a string into a list of substrings based on a specified delimiter. The delimiter can be a space, a comma, or any other character you choose. By default, it splits the string on whitespace (spaces, tabs, and newline characters). This method is particularly useful when you need to separate words or elements in a string.

Syntax:

list_of_strings = string.split([delimiter[, maxsplit]])

- string: This is the string that you want to split into substrings.

- delimiter (optional): This is an optional parameter that specifies the character or characters on which to split the string. If not provided, the string is split on whitespace by default.

- maxsplit (optional): This is an optional parameter that specifies the maximum number of splits to perform. If not provided, there is no maximum limit to the number of splits.

Example of Usage:

 # Example 1: Splitting on whitespace

text = "Hello World"

words = text.split()

print(words)

Output: ['Hello', 'World']

 # Example 2: Splitting on a specific character (comma)

csv_data = "apple,banana,orange"

fruits = csv_data.split(",")

print(fruits)

Output: ['apple', 'banana', 'orange']

 # Example 3: Using maxsplit to limit the number of splits

sentence = "I am learning Python programming"

words = sentence.split(" ", 2)

print(words)

Output: ['I', 'am', 'learning Python programming']

Explanation of the Examples:

1. In Example 1, the split() method splits the string text into a list of words based on the default delimiter (whitespace). The resulting list contains two words, "Hello" and "World."

2. In Example 2, the split() method is used to split a CSV data string (csv_data) into a list of fruits using a comma (",") as the delimiter.

3. In Example 3, the split() method is used with the maxsplit parameter set to 2. This limits the number of splits to 2, so the resulting list contains three elements, breaking the sentence into "I," "am," and "learning Python programming."

Tips:

- The split() method is very useful for processing text data, such as parsing CSV files or breaking sentences into words.

- By default, it splits on whitespace, but you can specify any character(s) as the delimiter.

- If you need to split a string into lines based on newline characters, you can use splitlines() instead.

- If you want to join a list of strings into a single string, you can use the join() method.

7.15 strip()

Description:

The strip() method in Python is used to remove leading and trailing whitespace (spaces, tabs, newline characters) from a string. This function is commonly used to clean up user input or manipulate text data by removing unnecessary spaces from the beginning and end of a string.

Syntax:

new_string = string.strip([characters])

- string: This is the string from which you want to remove leading and trailing characters.

- characters (optional): This is an optional parameter that specifies the characters to be removed from both the beginning and end of the string. If not provided, it defaults to removing whitespace.

Example of Usage:

 # Example 1: Removing leading and trailing whitespace

text = "   Hello, World!   "

cleaned_text = text.strip()

print(cleaned_text)

Output: "Hello, World!"

Example 2: Removing specific characters

text = "###Python###"

cleaned_text = text.strip("#")

print(cleaned_text)

Output: "Python"

Example 3: Removing specified characters from both ends

text = "ABCDEF123XYZ"

cleaned_text = text.strip("ABCXYZ")

print(cleaned_text)

Output: "DEF123"

Explanation of the Examples:

1. In Example 1, the strip() method removes the leading and trailing spaces from the string text. The resulting string is "Hello, World!" with no leading or trailing spaces.

2. In Example 2, the strip() method is used to remove the "#" characters from both ends of the string text. The resulting string is "Python."

3. In Example 3, the strip() method removes the specified characters ("A," "B," "C," "X," "Y," "Z") from both ends of the string text. The resulting string is "DEF123."

Tips:

- The strip() method is useful for cleaning up user input, especially when working with forms or text data.

- If you only want to remove leading whitespace, you can use the lstrip() method, and if you only want to remove trailing whitespace, you can use the rstrip() method.

- Be cautious when specifying characters to remove with the characters parameter, as it removes all occurrences of those characters from both ends of the string.

7.16 upper()

Description:

The upper() method in Python is used to convert all the characters in a string to uppercase. It is a string formatting function that can be used when you want to ensure that all characters in a string are in uppercase, regardless of their original case.

Syntax:

new_string = string.upper()

- string: This is the string whose characters you want to convert to uppercase.

The upper() method returns a new string with all characters converted to uppercase.

Example of Usage:

 # Example 1: Converting a string to uppercase

text = "Hello, World!"

uppercase_text = text.upper()

print(uppercase_text)

```python
# Output: "HELLO, WORLD!"
```

 # Example 2: Handling user input

```python
user_input = input("Enter your name: ")
formatted_name = user_input.strip().upper()
print("Hello, " + formatted_name + "!")
# Output: "Hello, JOHN!" (if the user enters "John")
```

Explanation of the Examples:

1. In Example 1, the upper() method is used to convert all characters in the string text to uppercase. The resulting string is "HELLO, WORLD!"

2. In Example 2, the upper() method is used to convert user input to uppercase. First, the strip() method is applied to remove leading and trailing whitespace from the user's input. Then, the upper() method is used to convert the input to uppercase. This ensures that the greeting message is displayed in uppercase, regardless of how the user enters their name.

Tips:

- The upper() method is useful for standardizing text data, such as converting input to a consistent case.

- If you want to convert a string to lowercase, you can use the lower() method instead.

- Keep in mind that the upper() method returns a new string with uppercase characters; it does not modify the original string.

VIII.
Programming Support Functions

8.1 compile()

Description:

The compile() function in Python is used to compile a source code string or a parsed AST (Abstract Syntax Tree) into a code object that can be executed by the Python interpreter. This function is primarily used for dynamic code execution, such as evaluating code entered by users at runtime or for creating Python bytecode from source code.

Syntax:

```
compiled_code = compile(source, filename, mode, flags=0, dont_inherit=False, optimize=-1)
```

- source: This is the source code string that you want to compile. It can also be a parsed AST.

- filename: This is an optional string that specifies the name of the file where the source code was read from. If not provided, you can use "<string>" for code entered as a string.

- mode: This is a string that specifies the compilation mode. Common values are "exec" for module-level code, "eval" for single expressions, and "single" for interactive statements.

- flags: This is an optional integer that can be used to pass additional flags. The default is 0.

- dont_inherit: An optional boolean that, if set to True, prevents the compiler from inheriting the built-in and global namespaces during compilation.

- optimize: An optional integer that controls the optimization level. The default value of -1 uses the default optimization level.

The compile() function returns a code object that can be executed using the exec() function or evaluated using the eval() function, depending on the compilation mode.

Examples of Usage:

1. Compiling and executing module-level code:

```python
source_code = """
def greet(name):
    return f"Hello, {name}!"

print(greet("Alice"))
"""

compiled_code = compile(source_code, "<string>", "exec")
exec(compiled_code)
# Output: Hello, Alice!
```

2. Compiling and evaluating a single expression:

```python
expression = "2 + 3"

compiled_expression = compile(expression, "<string>", "eval")

result = eval(compiled_expression)

print(result)

# Output: 5
```

Explanation of the Examples:

- In the first example, the compile() function is used to compile a Python module-level code represented as a string. The exec() function is then used to execute the compiled code, resulting in the "Hello, Alice!" output.

- In the second example, the compile() function is used to compile a single expression, "2 + 3." The eval() function is used to evaluate the compiled expression, and the result (5) is printed.

Tips:

- Be cautious when using the compile() function with untrusted input, as it can execute arbitrary code. Avoid using it with untrusted sources.

- The compile() function is commonly used in scenarios where dynamic code generation or execution is required, such as in REPL (Read-Eval-Print Loop) environments or interactive code editors.

8.2 eval()

Description:

The eval() function in Python is used to evaluate a single dynamically generated Python expression or a block of code that can be executed. It takes a string as input, interprets it as Python code, and then executes that code within the current execution context.

Syntax:

result = eval(expression, globals=None, locals=None)

- expression: This is a string containing the Python expression or code to be evaluated.

- globals (optional): This is a dictionary that represents the global symbol table. If provided, it will be used as the global namespace for evaluating the expression. If not specified, the current global namespace is used.

- locals (optional): This is a dictionary that represents the local symbol table. If provided, it will be used as the local namespace for evaluating the expression. If not specified, the current local namespace is used.

Examples of Usage:

1. Evaluating a simple mathematical expression:

```python
expression = "2 + 3"
result = eval(expression)
print(result)
# Output: 5
```

2. Evaluating an expression with variables:

```python
x = 10
y = 20
expression = "x + y"
result = eval(expression, globals(), locals())
print(result)
# Output: 30
```

Explanation of the Examples:

- In the first example, the eval() function evaluates the expression "2 + 3" and returns the result 5. The result is printed to the console.

- In the second example, variables x and y are defined in the global namespace, and the eval() function is used to evaluate the expression "x + y". The result is calculated within the provided global and local namespaces and is printed as 30.

Tips:

- Be cautious when using the eval() function with untrusted input, as it can execute arbitrary code. Avoid using it with untrusted sources.

- If you need to evaluate multiple statements or a block of code, consider using the exec() function instead of eval(), as exec() can handle multiple statements.

- It's recommended to pass explicit globals and locals dictionaries to control the namespaces in which the code is evaluated. This helps avoid unintended side effects and improves code safety.

8.3 exec()

Description:

The exec() function in Python is used for the dynamic execution of Python programs, which can either be a single statement or a block of statements. It allows you to execute code that is dynamically generated as a string. This function is often used when you want to execute Python code stored in a variable or read from an external source.

Syntax:

```
exec(object, globals=None, locals=None)
```

- object: This can be a string containing one or more valid Python statements that you want to execute. It can also be a code object (a compiled code representation), a file-like object, or an iterable of source code strings.

- globals (optional): This is a dictionary representing the global symbol table. If provided, it will be used as the global namespace for executing the code. If not specified, the current global namespace is used.

- locals (optional): This is a dictionary representing the local symbol table. If provided, it will be used as the local namespace for executing the code. If not specified, the current local namespace is used.

Examples of Usage:

1. Executing a single Python statement:

```python
code = "print('Hello, world!')"
exec(code)
# Output: Hello, world!
```

2. Executing a block of Python code:

```python
code = """
x = 10
y = 20
sum = x + y
print(sum)
"""
exec(code)
# Output: 30
```

Explanation of the Examples:

- In the first example, the exec() function is used to execute a single Python statement that prints "Hello, world!" to the console.

- In the second example, a block of Python code is provided as a string, and the exec() function executes it. This code defines variables x and y, calculates their sum, and prints the result.

Tips:

- Use the exec() function carefully, especially when executing code from untrusted sources, as it can execute arbitrary code.

- If you need to evaluate a single expression and obtain its value, consider using the eval() function instead of exec(). eval() returns the value of the expression, while exec() is used for executing code that may not have a return value.

- Be mindful of the namespaces (globals and locals) when using exec(). Explicitly passing these dictionaries can help control where variables are defined and modified within the code being executed.

- It's a good practice to minimize the use of exec() and eval() in your code, as they can make the code harder to understand and maintain.

8.4 help()

Description:

The help() function in Python is used to retrieve information about available objects, modules, functions, classes, and methods. It provides a built-in interactive help system that can be used to obtain documentation and information about Python entities. You can use help() to get documentation for modules, classes, functions, methods, keywords, and more.

Syntax:

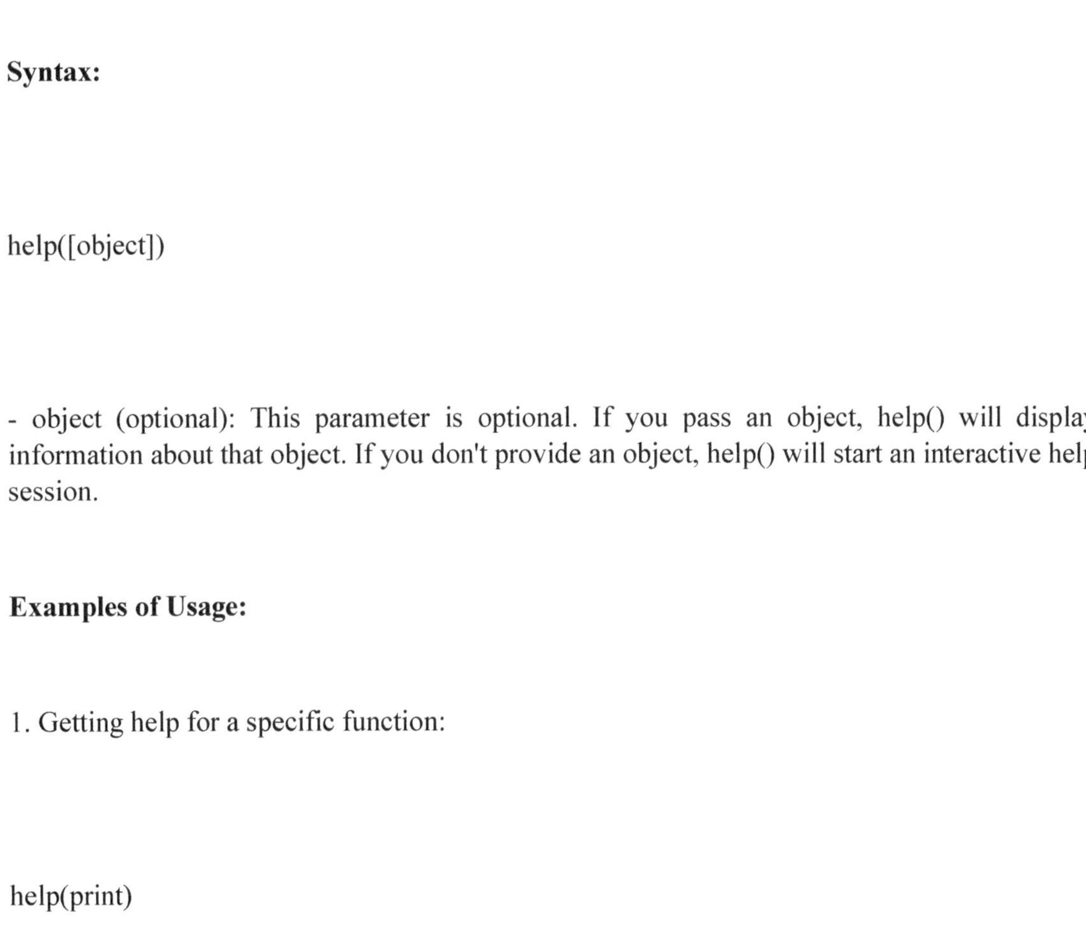

```
help([object])
```

- object (optional): This parameter is optional. If you pass an object, help() will display information about that object. If you don't provide an object, help() will start an interactive help session.

Examples of Usage:

1. Getting help for a specific function:

```
help(print)
```

This will display documentation about the print() function, including its usage and parameters.

2. Getting help for a module:

import math

help(math)

This will display documentation for the math module, including the functions and constants it provides.

3. Starting an interactive help session:

help()

This will start an interactive help session where you can enter the name of an object or topic to get information about it. To exit the interactive help session, press the q key.

Explanation of the Examples:

- In the first example, help(print) is used to get information about the print function. It displays documentation explaining how to use the print() function.

- In the second example, help(math) is used to get information about the math module. It displays documentation for the math module and lists the functions and constants it contains.

- The third example demonstrates how to start an interactive help session. Once inside the interactive session, you can type the name of an object or topic to get information about it. To exit the interactive session, press q.

Tips:

- The help() function is a valuable tool for exploring and learning about Python's built-in and user-defined objects. It can help you understand how to use various functions, modules, and classes effectively.

- When using the interactive help session, remember that you can navigate through the documentation using arrow keys and press q to exit.

- To access the Python documentation outside of the Python interpreter, you can use the pydoc command-line tool, which provides similar functionality to help(). For example, running pydoc math in the terminal will display documentation for the math module.

8.5 open()

Description:

The open() function in Python is used to open files and work with them. It allows you to perform various file operations such as reading, writing, and appending to files. The open() function returns a file object that you can use to interact with the file.

Syntax:

open(file, mode='r', buffering=-1, encoding=None, errors=None, newline=None, closefd=True, opener=None)

- file: The name of the file or a path to the file you want to open.

- mode (optional): A string that specifies the mode in which the file will be opened. The default mode is 'r' (read).

- buffering (optional): An integer that specifies the buffering policy. The default value is -1, which means the system default buffering policy will be used.

- encoding (optional): A string that specifies the encoding of the file. If not provided, the default encoding depends on the platform.

- errors (optional): A string that specifies how encoding and decoding errors should be handled. The default is None, which means errors will raise exceptions.

- newline (optional): A string that specifies how line endings should be handled. The default is None, which means universal newline mode is used.

- closefd (optional): A Boolean value that specifies whether to close the file descriptor when the file is closed. The default is True.

- opener (optional): A custom opener function for opening files. If not provided, the built-in open() function is used.

Examples of Usage:

1. Opening a file for reading:

file = open('example.txt', 'r')

This opens the file 'example.txt' in read mode and assigns the file object to the variable file.

2. Reading the contents of a file:

```
with open('example.txt', 'r') as file:
    content = file.read()
    print(content)
```

This opens 'example.txt' in read mode, reads its contents into the content variable, and then prints the content.

3. Writing to a file:

```python
with open('output.txt', 'w') as file:
    file.write('Hello, World!')
```

This opens 'output.txt' in write mode and writes the string 'Hello, World!' to the file.

Tips:

- Always use the with statement (context manager) when working with files. It ensures that the file is properly closed when you're done with it, even if an exception is raised.

- Be cautious when opening files in write ('w') mode, as it will overwrite the file if it already exists. To avoid data loss, consider using append ('a') mode or checking if the file exists before writing.

- Use the appropriate mode ('r' for reading, 'w' for writing, 'a' for appending) based on your intended file operation.

- Specify the encoding parameter when working with text files to ensure proper character encoding, especially when dealing with non-ASCII characters.

- To iterate over the lines of a text file, you can use a for loop or the readline() method in a loop.

8.6 print()

Description:

The print() function in Python is used to display messages, variables, or expressions to the console or standard output. It is a fundamental function for debugging, logging, and providing information to users in a Python program.

Syntax:

print(*objects, sep=' ', end='\n', file=sys.stdout, flush=False)

- objects (optional): One or more values, variables, or expressions that you want to print. You can separate multiple objects by commas.

- sep (optional): A string that specifies the separator between the printed objects. The default is a space (' ').

- end (optional): A string that specifies what should be printed at the end of the output. The default is a newline character ('\n').

- file (optional): A file-like object (e.g., a file, standard output) where the output will be printed. The default is sys.stdout, which is the console.

- flush (optional): A Boolean value that specifies whether the output buffer should be flushed. The default is False, which means the buffer is not flushed immediately.

Examples of Usage:

1. Printing a simple message:

```python
print("Hello, World!")
```

This will print the message "Hello, World!" to the console.

2. Printing variables and expressions:

```python
name = "Alice"
age = 30
print("Name:", name, "Age:", age)
```

This will print the values of the name and age variables along with labels.

3. Changing the separator and end character:

```python
print(1, 2, 3, sep=', ', end='!\n')
```

This will print the numbers 1, 2, and 3 separated by commas and ending with an exclamation mark.

Tips:

- You can use the sep parameter to customize the separator between printed objects. For example, setting sep='|' would print objects with a vertical bar separator.

- The end parameter allows you to specify what character(s) should appear at the end of the printed output. By default, it's a newline character, so each print() call starts on a new line.

- If you want to print to a file other than the console, you can specify a different file object using the file parameter. For example, file=open('output.txt', 'w') would print to a file named 'output.txt'.

- The flush parameter can be set to True if you want to force an immediate flush of the output buffer. This can be useful in situations where you want to ensure that the printed data is visible immediately.

IX.
Miscellaneous Functions

9.1 dir()

Description:

The dir() function in Python is used to list all the attributes (methods and properties) of an object, module, or namespace. It returns a list of names, representing the valid attributes for the given object.

Syntax:

dir([object])

- object (optional): An object, module, or namespace whose attributes you want to list. If not provided, dir() lists the attributes of the current scope or namespace.

Examples of Usage:

1. Listing attributes of a module:

```python
import math

attributes = dir(math)

print(attributes)
```

This code will list all the attributes (functions, constants, etc.) available in the math module.

2. Listing attributes of an object:

```python
class Person:
    def __init__(self, name, age):
        self.name = name
        self.age = age

person = Person("Alice", 30)
attributes = dir(person)
print(attributes)
```

This code will list the attributes of the person object, which include 'age' and 'name'.

3. Listing attributes of the current scope:

```python
def my_function():

    x = 10

    y = "Hello"

    attributes = dir()

    print(attributes)


my_function()
```

This code, when executed, will list the attributes in the scope of the my_function function, which includes 'x', 'y', and 'attributes'.

Tips:

- The dir() function is useful for inspecting the contents of objects, modules, or namespaces, making it a valuable tool for debugging and exploration.

- When used without any argument, dir() lists the attributes of the current namespace. This can be handy for checking what variables and functions are defined in the current scope.

- Keep in mind that dir() lists all attributes, including built-in ones, so the list can be quite extensive.

9.2 globals()

Description:

The globals() function in Python is used to return a dictionary containing the current global symbol table. It provides access to all global variables, functions, and classes that are defined in the current module or script.

Syntax:

```
globals()
```

Example of Usage:

```
# Create a global variable
global_var = 42

def my_function():
    # Access global_var from within the function
    global_var = globals()['global_var']
    print("Inside my_function, global_var is:", global_var)
```

```python
my_function()
print("Outside my_function, global_var is:", global_var)


# Accessing all global variables and functions
global_symbols = globals()
print(global_symbols)
```

Output:

```
Inside my_function, global_var is: 42

Outside my_function, global_var is: 42

{'__name__': '__main__', '__doc__': None, '__package__': None, '__loader__': <_frozen_importlib_external.SourceFileLoader object at 0x7f154437b1c0>, '__spec__': None, '__annotations__': {}, '__builtins__': <module 'builtins' (built-in)>, 'global_var': 42, 'my_function': <function my_function at 0x7f154438d160>, 'global_symbols': {...}}
```

In this example:

- We create a global variable named global_var and define a function my_function.

- Inside my_function, we use globals()['global_var'] to access the global variable global_var. This demonstrates how globals() can be used to access global symbols from within a function.

- We print the value of global_var both inside and outside the function to show that they are the same.

- Finally, we use globals() to access all the global symbols defined in the current module, including the variables global_var and my_function.

Tips:

- The globals() function is commonly used for debugging and introspection, especially when you need to access global variables or functions from within a function or when you want to list all global symbols defined in a module.

- While it's useful for introspection, it should be used sparingly in production code, as it can make code less readable and maintainable when global variables are accessed from various parts of a program. It's often better to use function parameters and return values to pass data between functions instead of relying heavily on global variables.

9.3 locals()

Description:

The locals() function in Python is used to return a dictionary containing the current local symbol table. It provides access to all local variables, functions, and classes that are defined within the current function or block of code.

Syntax:

locals()

Example of Usage:

```python
def my_function():
    local_var = 42
    local_symbols = locals()
    print("Local symbols inside my_function:", local_symbols)

my_function()
```

```python
# Attempting to access local_var outside the function raises a NameError
try:
    print(local_var)
except NameError as e:
    print("NameError:", e)
```

Output:

```
Local symbols inside my_function: {'local_var': 42}
NameError: name 'local_var' is not defined
```

In this example:

- We define a function my_function in which we create a local variable named local_var. Inside the function, we use locals() to access the local symbol table, which contains the variable local_var.

- We print the local symbols dictionary to see the contents of the local symbol table.

- When we attempt to access local_var outside the function, it raises a NameError because local_var is a local variable and is not defined in the global scope.

Tips:

- The locals() function is often used for introspection, debugging, and dynamically accessing local variables within a function or block of code.

- Keep in mind that modifying the dictionary returned by locals() does not affect the actual local variables. It provides a read-only view of the local symbol table. If you need to modify local variables, you should do so directly within the function's code.

- While locals() is a valuable tool for understanding the state of local variables, it should be used judiciously. Excessive reliance on introspection functions like locals() can make code less readable and harder to maintain. In most cases, it's better to pass data between functions using parameters and return values rather than relying heavily on global or local variables.

9.4 object()

Description:

In Python, the object() function returns a new featureless object. This function is a built-in constructor that returns a new instance of the base object class. The base object class is the root of the Python class hierarchy and serves as the base class for all other classes. When you call object(), it creates an empty, generic object with no attributes or methods.

Syntax:

object()

Example of Usage:

```
# Creating a new object using the object() constructor
new_object = object()

# Checking the type of the object
print(type(new_object))  # <class 'object'>
```

```python
# Attempting to access attributes or methods on the object
try:
    print(new_object.some_attribute)
except AttributeError as e:
    print("AttributeError:", e)
```

Output:

```
<class 'object'>
AttributeError: 'object' object has no attribute 'some_attribute'
```

In this example:

- We create a new object using the object() constructor and assign it to the variable new_object.

- We use the type() function to check the type of the new_object, which confirms that it is of type <class 'object'>.

- We attempt to access a non-existent attribute (some_attribute) on the object, which raises an AttributeError since the object created by object() has no attributes or methods.

Tips:

- The object() constructor is rarely used directly in Python code. Its primary purpose is to serve as a base class for creating other classes. Most Python objects inherit from object implicitly.

- The object class itself does not provide any useful methods or attributes, but it serves as the foundation for object-oriented programming in Python.

- When creating custom classes, you usually inherit from object or another suitable base class to define your own attributes and methods. For example:

```python
class MyCustomClass(object):
    def __init__(self, value):
        self.value = value
```

- The object() constructor can be helpful in certain advanced use cases, such as metaprogramming or creating objects dynamically, but it's not typically used in everyday Python programming.

9.5 range()

Description:

In Python, the range() function is used to create a sequence of numbers, typically used for iterating over a specific range of values in a for loop. It returns an immutable sequence of numbers between the given start, stop, and step values. The range() function can take one, two, or three arguments, specifying the start, stop, and step values for the sequence.

Syntax:

range(stop)

range(start, stop)

range(start, stop, step)

- start (optional): The starting value for the sequence (inclusive). If not provided, it defaults to 0.

- stop (required): The end value for the sequence (exclusive). The sequence stops before reaching this value.

- step (optional): The step value, which determines the spacing between values in the sequence. If not provided, it defaults to 1.

Example of Usage:

```python
# Using range() with one argument (stop)
for i in range(5):
    print(i)


# Using range() with two arguments (start, stop)
for j in range(2, 8):
    print(j)


# Using range() with three arguments (start, stop, step)
for k in range(1, 10, 2):
    print(k)
```

Output:

```
0
1
2
3
4
2
3
4
5
```

6

7

1

3

5

7

9

In this example:

- The first for loop uses range(5) to iterate over values from 0 to 4 (5 is the stop value), and it prints each value.

- The second for loop uses range(2, 8) to iterate over values from 2 to 7 (8 is the stop value), and it prints each value.

- The third for loop uses range(1, 10, 2) to iterate over odd values from 1 to 9 (10 is the stop value), with a step of 2, and it prints each value.

Tips:

- The range() function is commonly used with for loops to iterate over a sequence of numbers. It provides a more memory-efficient way of generating sequences compared to creating a list of numbers.

- Remember that the stop value is exclusive, meaning that the sequence stops before reaching that value. If you want the sequence to include the stop value, you may need to adjust it accordingly.

- If you omit the start argument, it defaults to 0. If you omit the step argument, it defaults to 1.

- You can convert a range object to a list using the list() constructor if you need the sequence of values as a list.

- In Python 2, the range() function returned a list, but in Python 3, it returns a range object. To get a list in Python 3, use list(range(...)).

- Be cautious when using large ranges, as they can consume a lot of memory. In such cases, consider using a generator expression or the range() function with a smaller step size to avoid excessive memory usage.

9.6 memoryview()

Description:

In Python, the memoryview() function returns a memory view object of the given argument. Memory views are a way to access the internal data of objects that support the buffer protocol (e.g., bytes, bytearray, and array.array) without making a copy. Memory views allow you to view and manipulate the data stored in these objects more efficiently.

Syntax:

memoryview(obj)

- obj (required): The object for which you want to create a memory view.

Example of Usage:

```
# Create a memory view of a bytes object
data = b'Hello, World!'
view = memoryview(data)

# Access and modify individual bytes in the memory view
view[0] = ord('h')
```

```python
view[7] = ord('w')

# Convert the memory view to a list
modified_data = list(view)

# Print the modified data
print(bytes(modified_data).decode())
```

Output:

```
hello, World!
```

Explanation:

In this example:

- We create a bytes object data containing the string 'Hello, World!'.

- We create a memory view view of the data object using memoryview(data).

- We use the memory view to directly access and modify individual bytes in the data object. For example, we change the first byte from 'H' to 'h' and the eighth byte from 'W' to 'w'.

- We convert the modified memory view back to a list modified_data using list(view).

- Finally, we convert the modified list back to a bytes object and print it, resulting in the string 'hello, World!'.

Tips:

- Memory views are particularly useful when working with large binary data, as they allow you to manipulate the data efficiently without creating unnecessary copies.

- Keep in mind that memory views provide a view into the original data, so any changes made through the memory view will affect the original object.

- Memory views are read-write by default, but you can make them read-only by using slicing. For example, view[:5] creates a read-only memory view of the first five bytes.

- Memory views can also be created from other memory views, enabling complex data manipulation operations.

- If you need to manipulate binary data stored in a buffer-like object efficiently, consider using memory views to avoid unnecessary memory overhead and improve performance.

X.
File I/O Functions

10.1 open()

Description:

In Python, the open() function is used for file input and output operations. It is the primary way to open and manipulate files in your Python programs. You can use it to open files for reading, writing, or appending data.

Syntax:

open(file, mode='r', buffering=-1, encoding=None, errors=None, newline=None, closefd=True, opener=None)

- file (required): The path to the file you want to open.

- mode (optional): The mode in which to open the file. It can be one of the following values:

  - 'r': Read (default) - opens the file for reading.

  - 'w': Write - opens the file for writing. Creates a new file if it doesn't exist or truncates the file if it exists.

  - 'x': Exclusive creation - opens the file for writing but fails if the file already exists.

- 'a': Append - opens the file for writing, but data is appended to the end of the file if it exists.

- 'b': Binary mode - if added to the mode, the file is treated in binary mode.

- 't': Text mode (default) - if added to the mode, the file is treated in text mode.

- '+': Update - opens the file for both reading and writing.

- buffering (optional): Sets the buffering policy. Pass 0 to disable buffering, 1 for line buffering, and any positive integer for buffer size. The default is -1, which uses the system's default buffering.

- encoding (optional): Specifies the character encoding of the file (e.g., 'utf-8', 'latin-1'). It's used when the file is opened in text mode.

- errors (optional): How to handle encoding and decoding errors, such as 'strict' (default), 'ignore', or 'replace'.

- newline (optional): Controls how newlines are handled when working with text files. Pass None to use the platform's default newline, '' for no conversion, '\n' for Unix-style, or '\r\n' for Windows-style.

- closefd (optional): A boolean value that specifies whether to close the file descriptor when the file is closed. The default is True.

- opener (optional): A custom opener function (advanced usage).

Example of Usage:

 # Example 1: Opening a file for reading

with open('example.txt', 'r') as file:

   content = file.read()

   print(content)

 # Example 2: Writing data to a file

```python
with open('new_file.txt', 'w') as file:

    file.write('Hello, World!')
```

Example 3: Appending data to an existing file

```python
with open('existing_file.txt', 'a') as file:

    file.write('\nAppending more data.')
```

Example 4: Reading lines from a file

```python
with open('example.txt', 'r') as file:

    lines = file.readlines()

    for line in lines:

        print(line.strip())
```

Tips:

- It's good practice to use the with statement (with open(...) as file) when working with files. This ensures that the file is properly closed when you're done, even if an exception is raised during execution.

- You can specify the full file path in the file argument to open files from specific directories. For example, 'path/to/myfile.txt'.

- In text mode (the default), reading and writing operations work with strings. In binary mode ('b'), they work with bytes.

- Use 'rb' and 'wb' for binary reading and writing, respectively.

- Be cautious when opening files in write ('w') mode, as it will overwrite the file's contents. Use append ('a') mode if you want to add data to an existing file.

- The newline parameter is essential when working with text files to ensure consistent handling of line endings across different platforms.

- Always close files when you're finished with them to free up system resources. The with statement automatically closes the file for you.

- If a file does not exist, using 'r' mode will raise a FileNotFoundError. You can handle this with a try...except block.

10.2 close()

Description:

In Python, the close() method is used to close an open file. When you open a file using the open() function, it's important to close it when you're done with it to release system resources and ensure that any changes made to the file are saved.

Syntax:

file.close()

- file: The file object that you want to close.

Example of Usage:

 # Example 1: Opening and closing a file

file = open('example.txt', 'r')

content = file.read()

file.close() # Close the file when you're done with it

print(content)

 # Example 2: Using the 'with' statement to automatically close a file

with open('example.txt', 'r') as file:

   content = file.read()

   # The file is automatically closed when you exit the 'with' block

print(content)

Tips:

- Always close files when you're finished with them to free up system resources and ensure that any pending changes are saved.

- The with statement is a convenient way to ensure that files are automatically closed when you exit the block, even if an exception is raised during execution.

- Attempting to perform operations on a closed file object will raise a ValueError. Always check if the file is open before performing any operations on it.

10.3 read()

Description:

In Python, the read() method is used to read the contents of a file. You can use this method to read the entire content of the file or specify the number of characters to read.

Syntax:

file.read(size)

- file: The file object that you want to read from.

- size (optional): The number of characters to read from the file. If not specified, it reads the entire file.

Example of Usage:

Suppose you have a file named example.txt with the following content:

Hello, World!

This is an example file.

Here are some examples of using the read() method:

 # Example 1: Reading the entire file

```python
with open('example.txt', 'r') as file:
    content = file.read()
print(content)
# Output:
# Hello, World!
# This is an example file.
```

 # Example 2: Reading a specific number of characters

```python
with open('example.txt', 'r') as file:
    partial_content = file.read(10)
print(partial_content)
# Output:
# Hello, Wor
```

 # Example 3: Reading the file line by line

```python
with open('example.txt', 'r') as file:
    lines = file.readlines()
```

for line in lines:

   print(line)

Output:

Hello, World!

This is an example file.

Tips:

- When you use the read() method without specifying the size, it reads the entire file.

- You can read the file line by line using the readlines() method or in a more memory-efficient way using a for loop.

- Be cautious when reading large files, as reading the entire content into memory at once can consume a lot of memory.

10.4 write()

Description:

In Python, the write() method is used to write data to a file. You can use this method to create a new file or append data to an existing file.

Syntax:

file.write(string)

- file: The file object that you want to write to.

- string: The data you want to write to the file, provided as a string.

Example of Usage:

Here are some examples of using the write() method:

 # Example 1: Creating a new file and writing data to it

with open('new_file.txt', 'w') as file:

    file.write('This is a new file created using Python.\n')

```
file.write('It contains multiple lines.\n')

    file.write('This is the last line.')
```

This code creates a new file named 'new_file.txt' and writes data to it.

Example 2: Appending data to an existing file

```
with open('existing_file.txt', 'a') as file:

    file.write('This data is appended to an existing file.\n')
```

This code appends data to the end of the file 'existing_file.txt'.

Example 3: Writing multiple lines using a list

```
lines = ['Line 1\n', 'Line 2\n', 'Line 3\n']

with open('multiple_lines.txt', 'w') as file:

    file.writelines(lines)
```

This code writes multiple lines to a file using the 'writelines()' method.

Tips:

- When opening a file in write mode ('w'), it will create a new file if it doesn't exist or overwrite the content of an existing file. Be cautious, as this will delete the existing file content.

- To append data to an existing file without overwriting its content, use append mode ('a').

- The write() method only accepts strings, so you may need to convert other data types to strings using str() before writing.

- When writing multiple lines, consider using a list of strings and the writelines() method for cleaner code.

10.5 seek()

Description:

The seek() method in Python is used to move the read/write pointer within a file to a specific position. This allows you to read or write data from or to a specific location within the file.

Syntax:

file.seek(offset, whence)

- file: The file object that you want to perform seek on.

- offset: The position to move to in the file. This is an integer representing how many bytes to move. The offset can be a positive or negative number.

- whence (optional): Specifies the starting point of the seek operation. There are three possible values:

  - 0 (default): Seek from the beginning of the file.

  - 1: Seek relative to the current position.

  - 2: Seek from the end of the file.

Example Usage:

Let's say you have a text file named "example.txt" with the following content:

This is line 1.

This is line 2.

This is line 3.

You want to move the file pointer to the beginning and read the first 10 characters:

```python
# Open the file in read mode
file = open("example.txt", "r")

# Move the pointer to the beginning
file.seek(0)

# Read the first 10 characters
data = file.read(10)

# Print the data
print(data)

# Close the file
file.close()
```

Output:

This is li

In this example, seek(0) moves the file pointer to the beginning, and read(10) reads the first 10 characters from the file.

Tips:

- Always remember to close the file using file.close() after using seek() to release system resources.

- Be cautious when using negative offsets or seeking from the end of the file to avoid unexpected behavior or errors.

10.6 readline()

Description:

The readline() method in Python is used for reading a single line from a file. It reads characters from the current file position until it encounters a newline character ('\n') or reaches the end of the file. The newline character at the end of the line is included in the returned string.

Syntax:

line = file.readline(size)

- file: The file object from which you want to read a line.

- size (optional): The maximum number of bytes to read. If not specified, it reads until the end of the current line.

Example Usage:

Suppose you have a text file named "example.txt" with the following content:

Line 1: Hello, World!

Line 2: This is a sample file.

Line 3: Python is great.

You can use readline() to read and print each line:

```python
# Open the file in read mode
file = open("example.txt", "r")

# Read and print each line
line1 = file.readline()
print(line1)

line2 = file.readline()
print(line2)

line3 = file.readline()
print(line3)

# Close the file
file.close()
```

Output:

Line 1: Hello, World!

Line 2: This is a sample file.

Line 3: Python is great.

In this example, readline() is used to read each line of the file one by one. The newline character ('\n') is included at the end of each line.

Tips:

- Be cautious when using readline() in a loop to read multiple lines, as it may lead to reading the entire file if not properly controlled.

- To read all lines of a file into a list, you can use file.readlines() instead of repeatedly calling readline().

- Always remember to close the file using file.close() after reading from it to release system resources. Consider using a with statement for better resource management.

10.7 flush()

Description:

The flush() method in Python is used to flush the internal buffer of a file. It ensures that any buffered data is written to the file immediately without waiting for the buffer to be filled or for the file to be closed. This is particularly useful when working with output files, as it helps in making sure that the data you have written is saved to the file.

Syntax:

```python
file.flush()
```

- file: The file object for which you want to flush the buffer.

Example Usage:

Suppose you have opened a file in write mode and you want to ensure that the data you've written is immediately saved to the file, even before closing it:

```python
# Open a file in write mode
file = open("example.txt", "w")
```

```python
# Write some data to the file
file.write("Hello, World!")


# Flush the buffer to save the data
file.flush()


# Close the file
file.close()
```

In this example, after writing "Hello, World!" to the file, file.flush() is called to ensure that the data is immediately saved to the file. This can be useful when you want to make sure that the data is persisted, especially in cases where the program may continue running and the file is not closed immediately.

Tips:

- The flush() method is typically used when you want to ensure that data is written to the file immediately, without waiting for the buffer to be filled or for the file to be closed.

- It is important to note that calling flush() too frequently can impact the performance of your program, so use it judiciously.

- In many cases, the file will be automatically flushed when it is closed, so explicitly calling flush() is not always necessary.

10.8 isatty()

Description:

The isatty() method in Python is used to check whether a file is associated with a terminal device or not. It returns True if the file is connected to a terminal, indicating that it's being used for interactive input or output, and False if it's not associated with a terminal.

Syntax:

file.isatty()

- file: The file object you want to check.

Example Usage:

Let's say you want to determine if a file is being used as a standard input or output for an interactive session:

```
# Open a file for reading
file = open("example.txt", "r")
```

Check if the file is associated with a terminal

if file.isatty():

    print("The file is connected to a terminal.")

else:

    print("The file is not connected to a terminal.")

Close the file

file.close()

In this example, the isatty() method is used to check if the file "example.txt" is connected to a terminal. Depending on the result, it prints whether the file is associated with a terminal or not.

Tips:

- The isatty() method is typically used to determine whether a file is being used for interactive input or output, such as when reading or writing to the console.

- It can be useful for handling file behavior differently based on whether the program is running interactively or as part of a script.

- When working with files that are not connected to a terminal (e.g., regular files), the isatty() method will return False.

10.9 truncate()

Description:

The truncate() method in Python is used to resize a file to a specified size in bytes. It can be applied to both text and binary files, and it works by either removing data from the end of the file to make it shorter or adding null bytes (zero bytes) to the end of the file to make it longer.

Syntax:

file.truncate(size=None)

- file: The file object you want to truncate.

- size (optional): The new size of the file in bytes. If not provided, it defaults to the current file position.

Example Usage:

Let's say you have a text file named "sample.txt" with the following content:

This is a sample text file.

It has multiple lines.

Let's truncate it.

You can use the truncate() method to shorten the file to a specific size:

```python
# Open the file in read-write mode
file = open("sample.txt", "r+")

# Read the current content of the file
content = file.read()
print("Original Content:")
print(content)

# Truncate the file to 25 bytes
file.truncate(25)

# Read and print the truncated content
file.seek(0)  # Move the file pointer to the beginning
truncated_content = file.read()
print("\nTruncated Content:")
print(truncated_content)
```

Close the file

file.close()

In this example, the truncate(25) method is called to shorten the file to 25 bytes from the current file position. As a result, only the first 25 bytes of the file content are retained, and the rest is removed.

Tips:

- When truncating a file, any data beyond the specified size will be lost.

- If the size argument is not provided, the truncate() method will default to truncating from the current file position to the end of the file.

- It's important to be cautious when using truncate() to avoid unintentional data loss, especially in scenarios where you want to resize a file. Always make sure you have a backup of the data or that the operation is reversible if needed.

CONCLUSION

In this comprehensive guide, we have delved into a plethora of Python functions, spanning diverse domains of Python programming. These functions provide essential tools for data manipulation, string formatting, file input/output, and much more. By mastering the descriptions, syntax, and usage examples provided for each function, you have acquired a valuable set of skills to enhance your Python programming proficiency.

Python is a versatile language, and understanding how to leverage these functions effectively is a significant step toward becoming a proficient Python programmer. Remember that practice is key to mastery, so don't hesitate to experiment with these functions in your own projects.

We sincerely appreciate your choice to purchase our book and invest in your Python knowledge. We hope this guide has been instrumental in your Python learning journey. If you have any inquiries or require further assistance, please don't hesitate to contact us. Your support and dedication to learning are greatly appreciated.

Thank You to Our Valued Readers:

We extend our heartfelt gratitude to all of our readers who have chosen to invest in our book. Your commitment to learning and enhancing your Python skills is commendable. We appreciate your trust in our content, and we hope that this book has provided you with valuable insights and knowledge that will serve you well in your programming endeavors.

Should you have any questions or require additional assistance, please do not hesitate to reach out to us. We wish you continued success in your Python programming journey and look forward to serving you in your future learning endeavors. Thank you once again for being a part of our community of learners.

THE END